SAGE RESEARCH PROGRESS SERIES IN CRIMINOLOGY
VOLUME 15

TABOOS in CRIMINOLOGY

Edited by **Edward Sagarin**

Published in cooperation with the
AMERICAN SOCIETY of CRIMINOLOGY

 SAGE PUBLICATIONS   Beverly Hills   London

Copyright © 1980 by Sage Publications, Inc.

For information address:

SAGE Publications, Inc.
275 South Beverly Drive
Beverly Hills, California 90212

SAGE Publications Ltd
28 Banner Street
London EC1Y 8QE, England

Printed in the United States of America

Library of Congress Cataloging in Publication Data

Main entry under title:

Taboos in criminology.

   (Sage research progress series in criminology ; v. 15)
   Bibliography: p.
   1. Crime and criminals—Research—Addresses, essays, lectures. 2. Criminal anthropology—Addresses, essays, lectures. I. Sagarin, Edward, 1913-   II. Series.
HV6024.5.T32   364.2   80-18175
ISBN 0-8039-1513-6
ISBN 0-8039-1514-4 (pbk.)

CONTENTS

Edward Sagarin

City College and City University of New York

TABOO SUBJECTS AND
TABOO VIEWPOINTS IN CRIMINOLOGY

Criminology is a social science, and since they are social scientists, it would appear at first glance that the pursuit of any relevant knowledge—or the expression and espousal of any viewpoint deduced from that accumulated knowledge— should never be off limits to criminologists. In this view, science is best pursued as research unfettered by ideology, restraints, or preconceived conclusions that one ardently desires to validate. Sometimes this means the expression of ideas that are out of favor with the powers that be, that are out of style with students and colleagues, and that, in the opinion of some, can only lead to socially damaging consequences. Scientists and other intellectuals have often scoffed at the cry of "dangerous ideas," dimissing the concept with the statement that ideas themselves can never be dangerous; only their suppression can be. Science, in this ideal and idyllic world, thrives in a free marketplace of intellects in conflict, where dialogue and clash occur in a public arena, and from which truth and truth alone will come forth, invariably victorious.

But, on more careful examination, this is a vision of science that bears little relationship to the world in which we live. Ideas, false and true, survive for long periods of time. There is no guarantee that, if false, they will eventually die; and even if this were so, while awaiting that eventuality, untold sufferings might be inflicted upon the world.

Yet, if we are to suppress ideas or, from the vantage point of the concept of taboo, just avoid them as untouchable and unmentionable because their consequences may be hurtful, are we not abandoning science in favor of ideology and advocacy? In so doing, are we not building on shoddy foundations that are certain to collapse because our social policy is derived from scientific fallacy?

TABOOS: THEIR MANIFESTATION IN CRIMINOLOGY

For the public, many topics have been beyond the realm of proper investigation. Death has been denied in a variety of ways: by the utilization of such euphemisms as "passing on" and "passing away," by the use of "if" and not "when" (pretending there is doubt as to the inevitability of the occurrence), by the invention of afterlife and reincarnation, and most recently by the brief flirtation of a few Americans with cryonics (Bryant and Snizek, 1973).[1] Suicide has been surrounded by an aura of shame, and sexual behavior was usually not a subject fit for a researcher. Homosexuality has had a peculiar history of taboos: first (and for a long time) denied and unmentionable, then indefensible, and still later deemed inappropriate for criticism and attack (compare Hooker, 1963, with Karlen, 1978).

All sciences, the physical as well as the social, have areas in which one must tread lightly, aware that something, whether can of worms or Pandora's box, is about to be opened and that the world is not ready to cope with the possible or foreseeable consequences. In criminology, it appears that a number of views—rather than subjects—have become increasingly delicate and sensitive, as if all those who espouse them were inherently evil, or at least stupidly insensitive to the consequences of their research. Thus, it takes courage to say what some of the proponents of unpopular views have said, or it takes unawareness of the logic of the position, or both. One cannot always be sure.

Unpopular beliefs arouse people's ire, which they manifest in a variety of ways. The case against their proponents, writes Adelson (1980), "is often made not by argument but by intimidation. To question these ideas [of the upholders of the accepted beliefs of the moment] is to risk jeers and hissing when the issues are discussed in public and a torrent of abusive letters when they are debated in print" (and more, and worse).

In the study of crime, the examples of unpopular orientations are many. Foremost is the link of crime to the factors of genes, biology, race, ethnicity, and religion. A biological predilection or disposition toward crime need not be hereditary, nor need it be present in one gene pool to a significantly greater extent than in another. In fact, most of the early work and a good deal of the latest and most sophisticated work on biological predisposition held race and ethnicity constant (see Goring, 1913; Hooton, 1939; Glueck and Glueck, 1950, 1956; Mednick and Christiansen, 1977). But the fact that the hereditary view of crime so easily becomes racial-ethnic (despite the tremendously different environmental conditions to which various groups are subjected) and the utilization of the biological orientation as an excuse for the rich and the powerful not to solve the crime problem by measures costly to the power structure, such as ameliorating the living conditions of the poor, have cast suspicion on those who espouse biological and even biosocial theory. While it would be far from accurate to say that the subject of biological predisposition to crime has been tabooed, it is probably correct to say that its upholders are often given short shrift, their ideas are dismissed with derision, and that they are in other ways subject to an informal collegial punishment, perhaps short of ostracism, but nonetheless unwelcome.

The problem of the relationship of race or ethnicity to crime has been much discussed. Yet those who contend that such a relationship exists and that it might be caused by other than oppression must be willing to withstand the charge that they are racist, anti-Semitic, and bigoted. Few countries are so homogeneous as single nation-states that there is no reflection of the differential crime rate among various ethnic and racial groups. In Europe, for many centuries, and until rather recently in human history, Jews were widely accused of the commission of certain horrendous crimes. In the United States, similar charges have been made against American Indians, blacks, Hispanic Americans—but, curiously enough, seldom is the issue of race and crime raised when one is discussing the crimes against these people committed by whites. Nor does this exhaust the list, for there are the Italian Americans, singled out for their alleged domination of organized crime; the Jews, accused of overrepresentation in white-collar and small-business crime, and more. That some of these subjects have been widely researched can be demonstrated beyond dispute, while others have been researched but little. However, an aura of suspicion follows those who would not only research the subjects, but come to a conclusion unsatisfactory to the defenders of equality and freedom; especially if they link their findings with heredity and not differential environment.

Nor is this the end of taboos in criminology. Others involve ideological goals, aims, and current fashions and trends. There is a response of scorn to anyone who suggests that marijuana use can be harmful, that homosexuality is abnormal or a symptom of a sickness, that feminism has given impetus and encouragement to female crime, and that men are sometimes deliberately and falsely accused of rape by women for a variety of reasons. All of these contentions are so offensive to various segments of the population that they are met with epithet rather than argument. This is not a new development, nor is it limited to criminology. Writing about the proposition that there are psychological differences between males and females, and stating "that these differences are worth thinking about," May (1980) adds that one who so much as raises the question is considered "at best mean-spirited and at worst a reactionary bigot." The words will be familiar to those who have raised the criminological issues mentioned earlier.

SOME LIMITS TO SCIENTIFIC RESEARCH

Science does set limits, or perhaps society does, through its governmental and intellectual worlds, on the propriety of scientific research. To pretend that there are no such limits, that all human knowledge is worth attaining regardless of the method of acquiring it or the consequences that will ensue, or that the scientist is only responsible for the knowledge and is not responsible—is, perhaps, irresponsible—for the consequences is to deny the real world in which we live.

Limits are set on the amount of and type of pain and suffering—with or without informed consent—that can be inflicted on other people to arrive at some anticipated finding. Many who do not deny the possibility of scientific knowledge emanating from work on animals nonetheless condemn electric shocks given to primates in order to determine the effects of pain on aggression (Curtis, 1978). We do not refrain from treating diseases in order that, by the use of radioactive and other techniques not previously available, we might trace the manner in which a given anomaly spreads within the body. If other forms of obtaining the information were unavailable, one would have to abandon the research.

Consequences, too, must be considered. For example, the cross-breeding of animals of different but closely related species, which on rare occasions brings forth a hybrid (almost invariably infertile) such as the tiglon or the liger, cannot be extended to humans and certain higher apes. No matter how much knowledge about evolution, the descent of man, or "missing links" might possibly emerge from such an experiment, the artificial insemination of a female gorilla with human sperm in the name of research is not something that can be countenanced. Nor would we want to breed a new species with the cerebral, vocal, and other capacities of the human and the strength of the gorilla, for science is not permitted free license to tamper with nature. There is no way to prove the contentions stated here, for they involve ethical choices on which I hope there is a consensus, but if one agrees that such research is impermissible, then one has conceded that there are indeed holds barred in the pursuit of knowledge and in the development of one's scientific research.

One cannot very well believe that all contraception is immoral (a view that I do not personally hold, but which is held by some eminent thinkers) and at the same time enter a laboratory and find it quite proper to engage in research on more effective ways of preventing conception. If one holds any moral values whatsoever (and it is assumed that everyone does), and if research is apparently and foreseeably aimed to assist in the destruction of those values or in undermining them, then such research should indeed be off limits. That the uses of research cannot always be foretold with accuracy is hardly mitigating, certainly not exculpating, for it is the duty of the researcher to make the effort to foresee them.

But, in criminology, is it possible that there will be such a foreseeable result in a direction that can be considered immoral? At this time, it might seem unlikely, although the history of our century would be lost to us if we did not consider the uses to which some information on race and biological superiority and inferiority has been put in the not very distant past.

THE FORUM AND THE RESPONSE

Certainly there is a difference between one researcher confronting another in the pages of a book or journal, or on the platform of a scientific meeting, and groups of people seeking to prevent points of view from being aired because they are distasteful to them. Students who have shouted down Shockley at universities and been unwilling to give him a forum for the elaboration of his ideas and gay demonstrators who have appeared at psychoanalytic meetings and made it impossible for scientists to offer their views on homosexuality (see Karlen, 1978) are treading on ground dangerously close to the imposed conformity and silence on controversial issues that was pervasive in the United States when Senator Joseph McCarthy was a powerful force on the national scene. But the complexities of these situations are many.

When a leading American publisher that had many scientists among its authors was about to bring out Velikovsky's *Worlds in Collision,* the scientist-authors gave their publisher an ultimatum: they would not continue their affiliation with a house that lent its imprint to such a work. The book did eventually come out, but only after the rights to it had been transferred (or perhaps sold, at a profit) to another company, whose authors were evidently not quite so fussy about the caliber of the names that accompanied their own in the catalogue. If one believes that *Worlds in Collision* was silly, amateurish, or wrongheaded, it becomes difficult to justify the measures that the scientists used, particularly bearing in mind the precedent that might have been set. Why not, instead, resort to response or argument, or just ignore the whole thing? But if one believes that it was a fraud, it seems quite proper that scientists should not want the imprint on their own works of a company that had been willing to capitalize on something of this sort. The use of the technique of ultimatum and boycott—of informal and, sometimes perhaps, formal pressure—appears justified. A notorious instance involves a book that pretended to tell the story of a human clone. The publisher, under pressure, hid behind a facade of advertising by asking: Is it fact or fiction?

The iconoclast is always welcome, and it is difficult to predict what ideas dismissed today as a claptrap might be accepted some years hence as establishment science. But this need not paralyze us in speaking out against anything that appears to us, at this stage of an ever-fluid body of knowledge, as absurd, wrong, dangerous, or fraudulent.

The works of Velikovsky and of the apparently fictional clone are far less inflammatory, however, and have far less potential for mischief, than some scientific research in criminology and other disciplines that is directed against and especially concerns entire groups. Shall such groups remain silenced? Shall they sit by if not offered a platform for rebuttal? Shall they relinquish their opportunities to demonstrate and, thus, their right of free speech? Shall they vote to have their tax dollars support research which they believe will inflict harm upon them? Shall they give support through tax exemption to groups sponsoring such research?

In criminology and other social sciences, research is usually conducted on or with human subjects. In a previous work (Sagarin, 1973), I suggested that some people have a right not to be researched. They are private people, not public; their privacy belongs to them, and their accountability is only to themselves. The research, no matter how noble the motives of the scientist who envisages himself above the battles, appears to the potential subjects as having more elements of risk and potential harm than of good. People are not minerals whose hardness is being tested, nor lifeless moons whose surface is being walked on for the first time in their existence. Subjects have no moral responsibility to cooperate with those who have come with their questionnaires, unless the subjects are public officials or other publicly accountable persons. Of course, scientists may arrive in disguise, but then they must take the consequences of the anger of those whose private space they have penetrated. So here there is a question of the taboo on research methods, rather than subjects or viewpoints. At any rate, research is circumscribed, notwithstanding the protests of those who say that in science no holds may be barred in research so long as we all pray at the altar of science.

To return to the irate students who would not give a platform to William Shockley, one is constantly reminded of the German professors whose classes were burst into by storm troopers in the period when Hitler was marching to power. It is an analogy that is slightly—but only slightly—valid. Shockley was not teaching, but was a guest on the lecture circuit (which is not to deny that professors have been prevented from teaching, that their classes have been invaded by conservatives and radicals, by pro- and anti-war elements, by Zionists and anti-Zionists, and many others). Victims of racial oppression are not storm troopers. Together with their new-found allies, when they shout down a Shockley, they are raising their voices as young men and women who have suffered, who have had slavery and lynchings in their own families, who have been systematically robbed and cheated in the name of biological superiority and racial inferiority. Nor is Shockley in the same camp as the German professors. He is a tragicomic figure who was awarded a Nobel prize for his work on transistors and who is no better trained in the field of genetics than is Jane Fonda in international diplomacy—but he is much more dangerous because he comes with scholarly pretensions rather than a pretty face.

In the case of the gay demonstrators, the problem has other complexities. That there has been discriminatory action, prejudice, bigotry, one can hardly deny. Certainly, the pro-gay people have gained platforms and public forums, but it is hardly in the interest of scientific dialogue to deny a forum to those who see the homosexual urge as coming from a pathology rather than a voluntary choice.

THE CAVEAT: GO SLOWLY, DANGER AHEAD

One of the scientific organizations, on taking a stand on freedom of research, has warned that those who espouse ideas or are doing research in fields where sensitivity is high ought to go slowly in coming to conclusions and in putting forth their findings. The history of the researchers on IQ and delinquency, IQ and crime, and on race, IQ and crime demonstrates anything but this. Investigators have rushed in headlong, with doubtful findings and with shabby research. If there has been a taboo, they have not been intimidated by it, but, on the contrary, have expressed confidence in doubtful work and have made deductions unwarranted by their own data.

It is a curious fact that one of the few examples of apparently fraudulent social science—like the Piltdown man fraud in anthropology, which was closer to physical science—was perpetrated by a scientist who was bringing forth his findings on the link between IQ and delinquency, namely, Cyril Burt. It may be to the credit of Jensen that he cast suspicion on the work of Burt (who had been knighted, an honor that Her Majesty has not yet seen fit to remove posthumously), but there has been no discussion as to why such a seemingly obvious correlation as IQ and delinquency—that is, the inverse correlation—required fraud to validate it. If the evidence is so striking and so overwhelming, why is it necessary for it to be fabricated out of the whole cloth, as in the work of Burt? I know of only one other instance in which the evidence that fraud had been perpetrated has been made so frequently and so convincingly against work in behavioral science. That is the charge against Rhine and the parapsychologists—and there the conclusion is almost inescapable that, without fraud, there would have been no evidence at all.

As late as 1972, Cortés, in a book in which he was striving to keep alive the delinquency and somatotype theories of William Sheldon, referred to Burt's "rather carefully controlled investigations," showing little skepticism toward work that was particularly undeserving of such praise.[2] In their enthusiasm, researchers betray their own ideologies, their will to believe. And they violate the elementary principle: Go slowly, this is ground fraught with potential danger.

Nor is Gordon more careful. I am grateful to him for the outstanding study of labeling and mental retardation (Gordon, 1975) that I had praised in public, for which he makes gracious acknowledgment (Sagarin and Montanino, 1976). But he hardly shows himself to be a scholar with scientific criteria when he cites Podhoretz to establish that the *New York Times* has an editorial opinion page heavily committed to the New Left (it is hard to say who is being more absurd, Podhoretz or the social scientist who relies on his work as if it were revealed gospel that did not require evidence of proof). His tale of woe concerning his difficulty in finding a publisher for one of his articles would be stronger evidence of the discriminatory practices of referees and editors venting their wrath against those who have unpopular or tabooed viewpoints if only the article itself were of impeccable quality. But the article published by Gordon (1976) in which he had "ample space and . . . did not have to contend with referees" is hardly an illustration of good social science or of responsible work—in fact, it is quite the opposite. Let us take a look at this work described (by Gordon himself, I might add) as having "emerged in the natural course of a long, systematic program of successful research on genuine scientific problems" (no one can say that immodesty is taboo).

Gordon, at great length and with considerable care, summarizes a number of studies on juvenile delinquency, all of which show a statistically significant higher proportion of black youths than whites who have had police contact, a juvenile delinquency record, commitment to a juvenile home, or who can be categorized as delinquent by some other criteria. Leaning on a wide variety of studies which he sometimes reinterprets to suit his own needs, and on experts who include, among others much more reliable, Shockley and Burt (and Shockley, in turn, is based upon Burt), Gordon weaves a connection between juvenile delinquency, race, IQ, and heredity that can be reduced to a number of simple propositions:

(1) black males have higher delinquency records than white males

(2) delinquents have lower IQs than other youths

(3) blacks have lower IQs than whites

(4) IQ is inherited, so low-IQ delinquents are likely to have low-IQ parents

(5) aside from the effect of the child's IQ on delinquency, there is the added effect of low-IQ parents being less effective socializing agents than high-IQ parents

I shall not here enter into an argument with this train of thought. Most of the statements in this chain are made with little or no validation. We have no empirical proof—or disproof—that low-IQ parents are ineffective socializing agents. We do not have evidence that low-IQ delinquents have low-IQ parents or that high-IQ delinquents (yes, there are such) have high-IQ parents. Perhaps it will be found that high-IQ delinquents have low-IQ parents. Either way the proposition is confirmed, because now the socializing thesis is called into play. We do not know whether high-IQ children or children of high-IQ parents have greater opportunities to escape official recognition as delinquents. The entire argument suffers from a lack of parsimony: Occam's razor has never been so dull as in the hands of Gordon.

But he may be right, after all. His impropriety is not in the investigation (if anything, it is in its absence, in the manner in which conjecture replaces research), but in the headlong rush into print with findings that are so tentative and, at the same time, so volatile. We are removed by too short a time from the evils that theories of racial inferiority wrought upon the black people in America, upon the Jewish people in Germany, and upon others for anyone to give us a signal to plunge ahead with new evidence that is still so tentative and flimsy.[3]

SCIENCE AND RESPONSIBILITY

Science is in search of truth, but the scientist must take responsibility, and must be accountable, for the foreseeable consequences of his search. The point was made clearly and forcefully by the distinguished philosopher of science Max Black (1975):

A more realistic conception of science *as it is* compels the claims of "neutrality" to be stigmatized as a myth and a pernicious one. The

responsibility for the consequences of scientific activity, in all its
interconnected aspects, rests squarely upon those engaged in it and
those who, directly or indirectly, support it.

Black writes that over every scientific laboratory should be
pasted the warning: "Danger: Scientist at Work." This is as true
of those who make correlations about crime as it is about those
who make napalm and other destructive weapons.

Nonetheless, there is a difference between the scientist
making correlations and the scientist making napalm, although
both actions may lead to unfortunate conclusions. One might
say that the latter is an inventor, the former is a discoverer. If the
scientist were not at work, the napalm would not be made, but
if the criminologist were not at work, this would in no way
change the objective social reality. The distinction is not always
clear-cut, and social reality is not always as objectively real as a
defoliated tree or a burning man, woman, or child. The scientist
who is attempting to explain what is already there cannot take
responsibility for what is being explained (that is, for the facts
that are brought to light), but must take responsibility for
bringing forth the explanation.

"Taboos are worthy admonitions," wrote Gordon Allport
(1963: p. ix), "but should not shackle free inquiry." They are
distasteful, he contended, but they are not without their logic.
And Farberow (1963: p. 4) stated, "When taboos continue or
develop *without useful society-enriching functions* or facilitate
self-defeating or self-destructive activities, questions should be
raised about them" (italics added).

Taboos in criminology, as in all fields of science, are undesirable, but criminology cannot pretend to a value-free
neutrality that sheds any vestige of responsibility. It must seek
the truth. Certainly, any distortion of the truth is invariably to
be condemned, but at the same time one must be aware of the
volatile nature of the material with which one is dealing, and
the responsible criminologist offers findings with special care
and circumspection when their potential for social harm is
great. If the researcher wishes to proceed (with admirable courage and, one hopes, slowly and responsibly), he can hardly
expect support from those who are his targets, those most likely

to be hurt from his work. On the contrary, he may find that people with low IQs are intelligent enough to spot an enemy robed in the lab coat made famous by science.

We are, in the end, confronted with ambivalent, ambiguous, and sometimes contradictory demands, not unlike those found by Merton (1976) in so many other facets of society and of social science. As scientists, we should always be in pursuit of knowledge and let the chips fall where they may; as citizens (or just residents or people), we should place restraints upon that pursuit in the interest of public safety and social policy. As scientists, we should work toward making that knowledge known to colleagues and others; as watchers of the American scene, we should be aware of the damage that may come from our work and take responsibility for the consequences that we should have been able to foresee. As scientists, we should conduct our studies without permitting our values to interfere with our findings; as people, we should live with our abiding values and seek to harness all of the institutions of society—including science—to work in the interests of those values.

Let those who would avoid research take responsibility for the consequences of that avoidance, but let those who would conduct the research likewise and equally assume responsibility for its consequences. That is what the problem of taboo in criminology involves.

NOTES

1. Cryonics refers to the practice of storing a recently deceased body at extremely low temperatures, where it would be preserved until such time as the cause of death could be cured by medical science. The body would then be thawed, and the person revived, before biochemical decay set in. It has never been taken seriously by scientists. The perfect experiment would involve a living person—not a dead one—held for a period in suspense at freezing temperature, but there have been no volunteers. Had there been serious scientific interest in cryonics, a mouse, rat, or guinea pig might have been used, but there is no record of anyone doing this.

2. There are two points that I should like to make. First, Cortés is very generous in praising people with whom he agrees. His book is filled with flattery, of which the reference to Burt is only a mild example. Second, he is here referring to some work of Burt that is not germane to the biology-IQ-delinquency controversy.

3. There is an example of such a signal given by Gordon when he points out that in Israel the Oriental Jews are more delinquent than the European Jews and that the former also have lower IQs. The phenomenon of differential delinquency rates is much better explained by culture conflict theory (see Shoham, 1966). However, in a land so beset by intergroup problems and other difficulties as Israel, the conjecture of Gordon could be just such a signal as I have described. Fortunately, it will not be, but only because it is more likely to be ignored.

REFERENCES

ADELSON, J. (1980) Review of "Sex and Fantasy," by R. May. New York Times Book Review (March 9): p. 3ff.

ALLPORT, G. W. (1963) "Foreword," pp. v-x in N. L. Farberow (ed.) Taboo Topics. New York: Atherton.

BLACK, M. (1975) "Is scientific neutrality a myth?" Delivered at the annual meeting of the American Association for Advancement of Science, New York, January 27.

BRYANT, C. D. and W. E. SNIZEK (1973) "The iceman cometh: the cryonics movement and frozen immortality." Society 11, 1: 56-61.

CORTÉS, J. B. (1972) Delinquency and Crime: A Biopsychosocial Approach. New York: Seminar Press.

CURTIS, P. (1978) "New debate over experimenting with animals." New York Times Magazine (December 31): p. 18ff.

FARBEROW, N. L. (1963) "Introduction," pp. 1-7 in Farberow (ed.) Taboo Topics. New York: Atherton.

GLUECK, S. and E. GLUECK (1950) Unraveling Juvenile Delinquency. Cambridge, MA: Harvard Univ. Press (for the Commonwealth Fund).

——— (1956) Physique and Delinquency. New York: Harper. (Reprinted in 1970 by Kraus Reprint.)

GORDON, R. A. (1975) "Examining labelling theory: the case of mental retardation," pp. 83-146 in W. R. Gove (ed.) The Labelling of Deviance: Evaluating a Perspective. Beverly Hills, CA: Sage Publications.

——— (1976) "Prevalence: the rare datum in delinquency measurement and its implication for the theory of delinquency," pp. 201-284 in M. W. Klein (ed.) The Juvenile Justice System. Beverly Hills, CA: Sage Publications.

GORING, C. (1913) The English Convict: A Statistical Study. London: His Majesty's Stationery Office. (Reprinted in 1972 by Patterson Smith.)

HOOKER, E. (1963) "Male homosexuality," pp. 44-55 in N. L. Farberow (ed.) Taboo Topics. New York: Atherton.

HOOTON, E. (1939) Crime and the Man. Cambridge, MA: Harvard University Press.

KARLEN, A. (1978) "Homosexuality: the scene and its students," pp. 223-248 in J. M. Henslin and E. Sagarin (eds.) The Sociology of Sex. New York: Schocken Books.

MAY, R. (1980) Sex and Fantasy: Patterns of Male and Female Development. New York: Norton.

MEDNICK, S. and K. O. CHRISTIANSEN [eds.] (1977) Biosocial Bases of Criminal Behavior. New York: Gardner Press.

MERTON, R. K. (1976) Sociological Ambivalence and Other Essays. New York: Macmillan.

SAGARIN, E. (1973) "The research setting and the right not to be researched." Social Problems 21: 52-64.

——— and F. MONTANINO (1976) "Anthologies and readers on deviance." Contemporary Sociology 5: 259-267.

SHOHAM, S. (1966) Crime and Social Deviation. Chicago: Regnery.

2

Michael E. Levin

City College of New York

SCIENCE WITH TABOOS:
An Inherent Contradiction

The best definition of science I know is P. W. Bridgman's: "Science is using your wits, no holds barred." It is not men in lab coats, nor cyclotrons, nor any special method. Certainly, some techniques—such as controlled experimentation and mathematical analysis—are characteristic of science, but in essence science is just the use of reason controlled by experience to discover how things are. Consequently, any kind of thinking and any fact is potentially relevant to any scientific inquiry, and the scientific mind is simply the open mind. In short, science with taboos is a contradiction in terms. Taboos are internalized, and hence especially insidious; they are restraints, not only on certain activities, but on thinking along certain lines and asking certain questions. They fence off areas as forbidden, evil, tainted. Taboos close the mind.

Examples of contemporary taboos abound. Environmentalism is sacred, so it is profane to ask if blacks are on the average less intelligent than whites. One mentions the crime rate of black adolescents with trepidation and apologies. Feminism, which has almost become our state religion, is similarly immune to scientific questioning. I have yet to see a psychosocial profile of the average feminist, despite the readiness of social scientists to analyze virtually any other group that appears on the public scene. Most discussions of innate male/female differences are prefaced by apologies to feminists and warnings about the irrelevance of such discussion to the goal of equality. Surely we have here genuflection, not scientific caution. And as these examples show, it does not take an external authority imposing tangible punishments to create a taboo. Anger from pressure groups and a scientist's own desire to "do the right thing" can create internalized inhibitions strong enough to amount to reflex aversion to certain topics.

What is distinctive and worrisome about taboos can be brought out by contrasting them with two legitimate constraints on scientific activity. The first one is: Conform your beliefs and behavior to the evidence. No responsible physicist would try to build a perpetual motion machine, but only because the evidence against perpetual motion is so great that any effort one might expend on such a project would more likely be better spent elsewhere. Now this is not taboo thinking. Reluctance to chase perpetual motion arises from assessment of evidence, not a general interdiction against perpetual motion or the marrow-deep sense that the omnipresence of friction is sacred. Perpetual motion occasions autonomous skepticism, not guilt or fear. A physicist will equably entertain the issue; he puts it out of court because he knows the answer already. Astrologers and circle squarers are mocked because their convictions are evidentially, not morally, disreputable. Now, while there are some who at least say that they regard the evidence against innate IQ differences between races as being as firm as the evidence against perpetual motion, it is hard to understand why they then bring such moral passion to putting the issue out of court. And no one can pretend that the evidence for the social etiology of sex differences is as decisive as the evidence for heliocentrism.

The second legitimate constraint on scientists is to conform to the general prohibitions of morality. I cannot rob you, even to finance a cyclotron. I am not permitted to ascertain certain facts about hematomas by braining you with a brick. If that is the only way to satisfy my curiosity, my curiosity must for the moment go unsatisfied. However, those who urge that inquiries about race and IQ, or the social impact of feminism ought not be pursued are urging more than adherence to general moral precepts. For not only are moral precepts not especially inquiry specific or science specific, they do not concern inquiry at all. They concern action. "Scientists shouldn't steal" is not a rule about scientists, but an application of the rule "Don't steal." It is a rule about actions, not questions. I stress this because confusion on this matter may be why certain lines of scientific research have been condemned as "morally wrong." Thus, if DNA research is excessively risky—if, as some alarmists have it, heedless biologists are about to infect mankind with a super-bug—it is wrong because it violates the general precept "don't create excessive risk," not because there is something intrinsically wrong with investigating DNA. Dangerous research is wrong for the same reason that the manufacture of nitroglycerine next door to a school is. And what would be wrong with risky DNA research would literally be the activities of using fragile test-tubes and installing leaky sealants, not the "activity" of wondering about DNA.

There should be no restrictions at all on the acquisition and dissemination of knowledge per se, no sacred theses that, like the letters of transit in *Casablanca,* "cannot even be questioned." Social conditioning should never be used to generate internal inhibitions in scientists, who should, on the contrary, be allowed by law and encouraged by the mood of the scientific and general community to pursue any question at all. Knowledge and curiosity are good, ignorance bad. The more we know, the better off we are and the better the world is.

The most obvious reason for permitting unlimited inquiry is that inhibition easily becomes a general habit of mind. Proscribing even a single area of inquiry establishes the precedent that *any* area *may* be proscribed and establishes the general principle that inquiry is not its own justification. Proscribing one question warns every scientist that his question may be the next on the Index. It is futile for the censor to dodge this consequence by offering a rational justification for his proscription. What he wants to create is a reflex aversion to certain thoughts, and he cannot do this if he is prepared to trot out reasons—for he then, in effect, readmits the whole subject to the realm of reason. Those who believe it is sinful to ask want to transfer the topics concerned from the realm of intellect to the realm of the viscera, and a show of reason on their part is bound to be spurious. However good a (nonscientific) reason someone gives for closing the mind about X, those interested in Y will inevitably realize how easy it would be to come up with an equally plausible reason for closing the mind about Y. If asking about X offends someone, can there be any ironclad guarantee that pursuing Y wherever it leads will not eventually offend someone? The Y-ologist knows he may be next, and thus is created the habit of worrying that your ideas may next be found to be off limits. If asking if women's liberation creates anomie "offends" feminists, perhaps tomorrow tabulating recidivism will "offend" criminals.

A look at history confirms the idea that scientific inquiry thrives only in an atmosphere of general intellectual freedom. Modern science emerged only when men felt free to question the doctrines of Aristotle and the church. Lysenko's ideological environmentalism ruined Russian genetics, and Communist China—where, until recently at least, the Marxist theory of society was holy writ—has yet to produce a fundamental scientific advance. The sacredness of a sociological tenet can inhibit theorizing about mesons because self-inhibition is a habit that makes the whole mind and the whole man hesitate. Granted, people can to some extent compartmentalize their thinking about different topics. This may partly explain the fairly high quality of Russian basic research. (Then, too, Russian physicists seem not to be especially bound by ideology. However, their track record is inferior to that of their colleagues in the Western democracies.) But this compartmentalization, when it occurs, is at best a holding action.

Research results can no more be adequately disseminated than attained in a taboo-ridden scientific community. One must wonder whether last month's provocative article will be this month's crime-think. In such a community no scientist can be sure that what he reads is complete or completely objective. Thus, I have heard some sociologists express skepticism about various experiments "demonstrating" the Pygmalion effect, since the pressure of environmentalism is so hard for scientists to buck. There are, again, general moral constraints on the publication as well as the conduct of research. A responsible scientist will not announce an easily misconstrued discovery via the *New York Times*. But admitting this in no way concedes that there is ever anything wrong with promulgating discoveries in the professional literature or explaining them carefully to the mass media.

There are two more positive arguments for unlimited inquiry that seem to be decisive. The first is that the truth on any matter will eventually make itself felt and known anyway. We do ourselves no favor by foregoing the pursuit of truth, because truth is pursuing us. If an ostrich can avoid the dingo by burying his head, he should do so. But as things are, the dingo will reveal himself to the ostrich whether or not the ostrich wants to know about him. The ostrich may never acknowledge in just those words (so to speak) that a dingo is after him, but the consequences of this fact—the dingo's bite—will be unaltered, and the ostrich's obliviousness will not help him when he meets these consequences. Unpleasant truths and their implications cannot be staved off forever. We should explore the facts about crime and feminism, race and IQ, and anything else, since the attempt to ignore them will fail. If, say, As are better than Bs at mathematics, there will never be as many competent B mathematicians, whether we like it or not. Reality is not so considerate as to let our plans succeed no matter what. A physiologist who has evidence that women differ innately from men may suppress this information because he believes its dissemination will frustrate the goal of equality. But the goal might be shown to be unattainable, and its pursuit foolish, by the very facts he is suppressing: It is not as if there were unconditionally desirable goals that would be frustrated by publication of information arrived at scientifically.

I have by now touched on the second reason for uninhibited inquiry: No matter what you want, you are more likely to get it if you know the facts. Suppose we want to use our educational resources most efficiently. It will clearly be useful to know whether members of group A are better than members of group B at mathematics. (I pick an example from education only because the topic is so much in vogue.) If, not knowing the facts, we simply assume that mathematical ability is distributed randomly, we will find to our dismay that expending equal energy in teaching mathematics to As and Bs produces relatively fewer B mathematicians—and we will not know why. We might then double our investment in training Bs. But if we knew beforehand that producing a "proportionate" number of B mathematicians was either impossible or would require an outlay of 5% of the GNP, we would clearly be in a better position to decide what to do next than if we had no idea whether we could succeed or not. When in the dark, we would always have to allow for the possibility that one more small outlay might do the trick. And remember that an alleged social good ceases to be perceived as such when it is seen to conflict with reality. If identical treatment of the sexes produces a psychologically disturbed generation, such treatment will come to be regarded as foolish.

When, as they will, plans go awry, we will have to decide how to investigate the causes of failure. If we are intimidated into assuming that the failure of Bs at mathematics is due to an environmental factor, we risk squandering funds on useless remediation or foredoomed research into the environmental causes of failure. A good example of this sort of obscurantism occurs in the report of the government panel on falling SAT scores, which ruled out a priori the possibility that girls' SAT math scores are lower than boys' because they are not as good at mathematics, and recommended changes in "role models" to boost the math SATs. If the discrepancy is due to innate factors, the government has opened an unpluggable drain on funds to raise SAT scores. Obviously (see Appendix), if the cost of research is low, we maximize expected utility by asking first if environmental remediation is possible. Failure to ask is not open-mindedness, but commitment by default to the environmental hypothesis.

My general point is quite simple: It is irrational to act under uncertainty when a small outlay can decrease uncertainty. Consider a hungry man facing two locked rooms, one of which contains food and one which contains nothing. It will take much effort to open either door, and the man has the energy to open only one. Suppose he can find out, by a small expenditure of his limited reserves, which door hides the food. It would be utterly daft for him to choose risking a useless effort to making this preliminary inquiry. But if he thinks it is wrong, wicked, unprogressive, elitist, racist, sexist, ageist, speciesist, or doorist to ask which door hides the food, he will be condemned to act irrationally and be more likely to starve.

Let me emphasize that, in general, I distrust any central goal-choosing and resource-allocating authority, favoring instead the Jeffersonian state in which each man pursues happiness without governmental help or hindrance. But if the government insists on allocating resources to achieve goals it itself has set—a habit our government has gotten into—it should do so in the light of the best possible information, even if the information makes some of us squirm. In one of its pronouncements, HEW declares that all talents are randomly distributed across all populations and implies that any disproportionate representation of a population must be due to discrimination. Now, we all know the kind of pressure that HEW can bring on its unlucky targets. But HEW offers no evidence for its proclamation, and many people evidently feel that to demand any evidence is to invite a curse. Yet, if HEW's assumption is false, the financial and human costs of affirmative action are dead losses. Incredibly, there are writers like Noam Chomsky who advocate greater governmental involvement in society's affairs while opposing any examination of the environmentalist assumptions that now control the direction of this involvement.

Admittedly, the cost of research involves more than money, and some fear that certain kinds of research, even if carried out in good faith, invite abuse. The simple reply to this is that any research can be abused. Ideological pressure can frustrate faithful research, as it did in the Lysenko affair, and ideologues can exploit even faithful research by insisting, long and loudly, on a link between it and some favorite world view. In the 1950s, Russia tried to parlay Sputnik into a vindication of socialism. The only thing to do to counter such abuse in an open society is to let research continue and to point out as often as necessary the gap between specific scientific facts and ideology. Interested parties should be restrained from interfering with research when such parties include well-intentioned meddlers as well as the cardboard "racists" of current demonology. The justification for adopting this posture is not merely that truth will out. It is also that the consequences of interference may be worse than those of unimpeded research. No one can know in advance what the upshot of an investigation will be; that, after all, is why one investigates.

But what if we can foresee that some pending research will have distressing consequences? The psychological harm done to members of groups found to be innately less intelligent, for example, might be considered an unacceptable price to pay for such knowledge. Indeed, even if the apparent deficiencies in the group's performance that motivated the research are eventually dismissed or explained environmentally, did not the mere raising of the question create a presumption that the group especially merited scrutiny, a presumption which itself has unacceptable sociopsychological consequences? I grant that declaring a group to be statistically underendowed with some generally prized ability will lower the self-esteem of that group's members. (Even if microsurgery could then be used to upgrade the intelligence of that group, everyone else would rightly demand an "intelligence-lift," and group differences would persist.) So what? Some clever neurologist will one day explain the viewer's response to Rembrandt's *Nathan Admonishing David,* and a little magic will have fled the world. Art lovers will be the poorer, but preserving the mystery of the aesthetic response is surely too high a price to pay for inhibiting science! Whether it hurts our sensibilities or not, truth will out. If Bs are of lower than average intelligence, pious silence will preserve no one's ego. This lower intelligence will still manifest itself in the all-too-frequent failure of Bs at those tasks whose performance requires intelligence and in the failure of society's efforts to rectify this failure. Such repeated frustration will eventually erode the self-esteem of Bs just as surely as explicit acknowledgement of an intelligence deficit. The long run accumulation of glancing blows is just as demoralizing as a direct assault on the ego.

When thinking about the feelings of certain privileged minorities (not the aesthetes), one tends to suppose that the obligation not to shatter self-esteem is absolute. This is a mistake. An academic advisor who knows that a student is incapable of graduate study should tell him so. If the advisor softens the blow by mentioning such specious factors as a tough job market, he should scold himself for cowardice. Nor does the moral urgency of honesty derive only from the beneficial results of saving the student wasted years. Truthfulness may have such results, but it may also be ignored or trigger a nervous breakdown. Moral common sense dictates that the advisor level with the student in any case, whatever the most probable net upshot in hurt feelings. Moreover, as this example brings out, there is a vast difference between harming with intent and allowing harm to happen as a known consequence of action done from other—and possibly unobjectionable—motives. The advisor we have been discussing cannot legitimately be compared to one who breaks bad news in order to see students crumble. Scientists investigating facts that may prove embarrassing are only as culpable as our good-faith advisor.

It is tempting to say that one is as responsible for the foreseeable harm of one's action as one is for the action itself or its intended consequences, but this is not so. Suppose I know that by moving slightly to my left (perhaps to get a better view of the Liberty Bell) I will reveal an old lady hiding from a mugger who is sure to attack her if he sees her. If I do so move, I am surely not as responsible for the harm that befalls her as I would have been had I actually assaulted her, even if my action guarantees that she will be harmed, and even if I know this. The point is one to emphasize. Many social scientists, particularly those of Marxist persuasion, tend to identify the purpose (or "objective" purpose) of a social practice with its consequences. For instance, if a certain bit of sociological research causes the cancellation of funds for some project, they might tend to say that the purpose or function of the research was the cancellation of funds (to cement the hegemony of the oppressors, no doubt). But the known consequences of an act are not, in general, that act's purpose: Purpose is determined by intent. I stress this seemingly verbal matter because ordinary moral intuition does consider the purpose of an act in evaluating it and in judging the responsibility of its agent. Let us refuse to surrender the pivotal word "purpose," and if we must surrender it, let us stress that "purpose" as used by functionalists is an equivocation on "purpose" as used in morality.

Granted, everyone—and hence every scientist—is to some extent responsible for the foreseeable consequences of his actions. But such responsibility diminishes rapidly as foresight becomes uncertain and the "last clear chance" to realize these consequences lies with others. When evaluating action in terms of unintended consequences, we quickly fall back on the criterion of utility: One must balance the problematic bad consequences of research against both the value of the particular bit of research and the overall harm done by suppressing any research. (Bear in mind, incidentally, that the harm in question involves hurt feelings, not any physical injury.) And history and common sense indicate that there is more harm in treating any empirical tenet as sacred and basing our actions on its sanctity than in keeping an open mind.

I have not explicitly challenged the existence of a right of people not to have their self-esteem or pet beliefs tampered with or the right of people not to have embarrassing questions asked about them. Certainly, the issue of freedom of inquiry is often framed in terms of rights: Philosophers have recently detected a "right to self-respect" and begun drawing some startling consequences from it. A few years ago the matter was purely academic, but it is so no longer. Having already restricted the funding of research that involves human subjects (and "marine mammals"!), the government may refuse to fund research on the crime rate of black adolescents—and penalize institutions that do support such research—because it violates somebody's "right" to self-respect. I am very skeptical about such rights. While I may have an obligation not to insult you, you have no corresponding right not to feel bad. You have at most the right not to be insulted. If information you would rather not have known becomes public as a consequence of the uninhibited pursuit of knowledge, nobody has violated your rights. The asymmetry becomes clear when you consider the parallels with killing and letting die. I violate your rights if I murder you, but no one violates your rights if you die of starvation because I sent someone else a CARE package.

But, even if one insists on this empty and pernicious talk of "rights" violated by scientific discoveries, the situation need not be regarded as one of right versus utility. People presumably have a right to expect that those who allocate resources gathered through taxes do so on the basis of the best possible information. The more managed an economy is, the heavier is the obligation on the managers to determine the needs and abilities of everyone managed. The population would be irate if the Department of Defense defended its ordering of a new missile, without having tested a prototype, on the grounds that an unsuccessful test flight would damage the self-esteem of its designer and his whole family or that interested parties might twist any negative results. And the chief irony would be that the government's ostrichlike attitude would not protect the designer. A defective missile will disintegrate when it is used: The designer will be humiliated anyway, and the public will be out millions of dollars with nothing to show for it. True, if God gave us His word that the missile would never be used, we could afford to treat the design as sacred and condemn anyone who questioned it as wicked. But that is not how the world is.

Quite apart from the public's right to get what it pays for, does not the private scientist have a right to free discussion, thought, and inquiry? One might, of course, simply deny that there are such rights; but, then, where did the far more obscure right to self-esteem come from?

Truth is good because it makes us more the masters of our fate and more apt to get what we want. Every little bit of truth makes us freer; not necessarily happier in the short run, not necessarily more pleased with ourselves, but freer. And that is why there should be no sacred ground that a scientist cannot trespass, even in his mind.

APPENDIX

Let R be the act of remediating, $\overline{R}$ the act of omitting remediation, E the hypothesis that environment is causing B's poor performance, and $\overline{E}$ the denial of E. Consider M_1, the matrix which lists the payoffs of each act under each hypothesis:

	R	$\overline{R}$
E	90	−90
$\overline{E}$	−10	10

$$p(E) = p(\overline{E}) = .5$$

Thus, for instance, we suppose that the payoff (R,E) of doing R if E is true is 90 (million dollars, say). Let us also suppose that we are ignorant about E, so that for us the probability $p(\overline{E})$ of E = $p(\overline{E})$, that is, the probability of $\overline{E}$, = .5. Then, if we use M_1 (including its associated probability assignments), the expected utility e(R) of doing R is 40, and $e(\overline{R})$ = −40. So if we use M_1, the rational thing to do is R. Now, in reality, E is either true or false. If E is true, p(E) = 1 and $p(\overline{E})$ = 0. Replacing the probabilities of M_1 by these values gives us matrix M_2:

	R	$\overline{R}$
E	90	−90
$\overline{E}$	−10	10

$p(E) = 1$
$p(\overline{E}) = 0$

It is easy to see that, if we use M_2 again, e(R) > e(R). Now let M_3 be the result of assuming that E is false:

	R	$\overline{R}$
E	90	−90
$\overline{E}$	−10	10

$p(E) = 0$
$p(\overline{E}) = 1$

If we use M_3 to compute expectation, it is obvious that $e(\overline{R})$ > e(R), so that M_3 tells us to do $\overline{R}$. Now let I be the act of investigating whether E is true and $\bar{I}$ the "act" of refraining from investigating. Matrix M_4 below represents the payoffs for each act given the world states E, $\bar{E}$. The payoffs are matrices: If we perform I and E is true (and our discovery procedure is reliable), the "payoff" is the use of M_2 to decide about R, and so on:

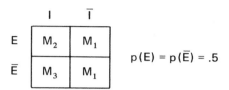

$$p(E) = p(\bar{E}) = .5$$

If we assume that, prior to investigation, the probabilities of E and $\bar{E}$ are both .5, several facts emerge. First, note that $e(I) = p(M_2)u(M_2) + p(M_3)u(M_3)$, where $p(M_i)$ is the probability that we will use matrix M_i and $u(M_i)$ is the value of using matrix M_i. Now, clearly, $u(M_i)$ is precisely the value of the action M_i tells you to do. Since M_2 tells you to do R, $u(M_2)$ = the utility of doing R in case E is true; i.e., (R,E), i.e., 90. Since we are assuming prior equiprobabilities for E and $\bar{E}$, $p(M_2) = p(M_3) = .5$. Likewise for the second summand in $e(I)$; $e(I)$ works out to be 45 + 5 = 50. However, performing $\bar{I}$ means choosing to utilize matrix M_1 *in any case*; i.e., doing R in any case. This is so because not investigating amounts to assuming that $p(E) = p(\bar{E})$. And the expectation $e(\bar{I})$ of such a course is easily seen to be 45 – 5 = 40. So $e(I) > e(\bar{I})$. So, if the cost of investigating is negligible compared to the payoffs at issue, I is the rational course of action. Notice as well that not investigating commits us to acting as if we believed the environmental hypothesis, since it tells us to do in any case exactly what we would do if we knew E to be true.

Like any formalization, this one must begin from some unargued assumptions. I have assumed that rationality dictates the maximization of expectation. The payoffs under I in M_4 should really have the form $M_1 - c(I)$, where $c(I)$ is the cost of investigation; I have assumed that $c(I)$ is negligible. I am assuming that the cost of R is nearly an order of magnitude lower than the benefits of R, given the environmental hypothesis. Obviously, the probabilities assigned to E and $\bar{E}$ in the "state of ignorance" matrix M_1 need not be equal, since there might be indirect reasons to prefer one over the other. However, I do not think that one need accept this formalization to be convinced of the intuitive point that it pays to investigate, and in any case the assumptions I have made seem to me realistic. What needs doing in the way of formalizing is a statement of the general conditions on E, R and (R,E) and their negations under which $e(I) \geqslant e(\bar{I})$. Two results at random: In the present example $e(I) = e(\bar{I})$ if $c(I) = 10$; and, generally, $e(I) = e(\bar{I})$ if $(\bar{R},E) = (\bar{R},\bar{E}) = -(R,E) = -(R,\bar{E})$. That is, even if the cost of investigating is as high as the cost of remediation, or remediation will get you what failure to remediate will lose you in any case, it is as prudent to investigate as not. In particular, $e(I) = e(\bar{I})$ if $(\bar{R},\bar{E}) = -(\bar{R},E)$.

3

Robert A. Gordon

Johns Hopkins University

RESEARCH ON IQ, RACE, AND DELINQUENCY:
Taboo or Not Taboo?

In preparing this article, I have interpreted my assignment to be one of relating and reflecting on observations I have accumulated as a researcher of what some consider a taboo topic. I shall try to steer a course somewhere between mere gossip and participant observation. First, I shall describe how my research led me to become involved with a topic that others regard as taboo, and some of the problems this has caused. I shall try also not to overlook some practical advantages that mitigate the disadvantages. Then, I shall examine some of the reasons that topics such as mine are considered taboo and assess their validity, culminating with a review of the empirical evidence concerning the assumption that lower IQ places a group at greater risk of genocide.

SCIENTIFIC ORIGINS OF MY RECENT RESEARCH AND SOME OF THE PROBLEMS I HAVE ENCOUNTERED

Ever since 1964 or so, I have been intensely concerned with the true relation between social class (or status) and delinquency. Everything I saw as a person pointed to a negative correlation, yet this was denied by influential works in the sociological and criminological literature.

A minor theory I had put forth in my dissertation (Gordon, 1963; later published as Gordon, 1967a) argued that something I called "social disability" was inversely related to social class.

"Social disability" was simply a blanket term for interpersonal and intellectual handicaps that reached such a level in lowermost social strata as to undermine social cohesion and render complex organizational undertakings impossible. As a social psychologist interested in small groups, I saw the activities of delinquent gangs, including the strife between them, as low-level mechanisms for generating social rewards that would be facilitated rather than impeded by the individual handicaps of their members. I found support for this approach in empirical data showing an inverse relation between social class and official delinquency rates and in general social psychological theory. However, I also was aware that there were obvious inconsistencies between my hypotheses concerning the relation between delinquency and certain variables and other claims in the literature. As is normal in science, I turned to examining the empirical evidence for those other claims that constituted foci of tension in my nomological network.

One of these troubling claims was the conclusion by Schuessler and Cressey (1950) that there was no relationship between personality disturbance and juvenile delinquency. I spent several years examining the vast literature they had reviewed and became convinced that they had misinterpreted the evidence, which pointed unambiguously to the opposite conclusion. (Someday I hope to publish these results, which taught me something about the state of social science and gave me confidence in my own scientific intuition.)

Simultaneously, I began to examine the ecological studies by Lander (1954) and others that had cast doubt on the relation between even official delinquency rates and socioeconomic status. In several publications (Gordon, 1967b, 1968a, 1968b), I demonstrated—to my own satisfaction, at least—that the ecological evidence actually demonstrated a strong inverse relation between these key variables that was quite consistent with my social disability thesis.

The third and final body of troubling research consisted of self-report studies, which claimed that when individuals provided data on their own criminality, no relation with social class is found. The discrepancy between such results and official delinquency statistics, which did show such a relation in ecological and other studies, eventually came to be widely regarded as evidence of social discrimination on the part of agents of the justice system.

As many of us have recognized (e.g., Reiss, 1975), a key factor in this ostensible discrepancy is the mildness of the kinds of delinquency reflected in the items of self-report instruments. But there is an additional, closely related consideration having to do with how many delinquents it would be reasonable to expect in the samples used in self-report studies. To address this question (which I do not spell out here), one requires a statistic that has been called the "prevalence" of delinquency, and one requires it for whites specifically, since most self-report studies have been performed on whites.

Consequently, when I turned my attention back to the self-report problem in the late 1960s and began writing a book on that topic, I searched for data that would reveal the proportion of individuals who become delinquent by a given age according to official criteria—what I and others call "prevalence," but what some have called "lifetime prevalence" (Leighton et al., 1963: 118; Lapouse, 1967). My work until then indicated that with the help of this additional information the self-report issue would be completely resolved, except for idiosyncratic methodological aspects of individual studies. Prevalence, it should be noted, is a widely recognized epidemiological statistic that often provides information of both practical and theoretical significance. In the area of illicit drug use and opiate addiction, for example, prevalence (or a closely related version of it) is needed, according to Greene (1974: 1), to assess:

(1) the amount of money and manpower needed to cope with the problem

(2) the effectiveness of a community's response to the problem, especially as reflected in changing rates over time

(3) the comparative needs of different areas when it becomes necessary to distribute scarce resources

(4) the effectiveness of various programs aimed at controlling the problem

(5) the relevance of various theories of the causes of the problem.

Not surprisingly, many surveys of the prevalence of illicit drug use have been published in recent years.

Against this background, one would have thought that studies of the prevalence of delinquency would also exist, and if they did not, that they would have received a friendly reception from scientists when performed. But the only existing study contained an error, and when, with a coauthor, I attempted to publish a correction as well as new estimates of prevalence from existing data, the work did not receive a neutral hearing on balance, let alone a friendly one. Rejections accumulated from one journal after another. The problem, apparently, was that the papers included, of necessity, race-specific as well as sex-specific rates, and these rates showed blacks to have much higher delinquency rates than whites.

All of these journal rejections came at a delicate stage in my career, incidentally, since I was involved at the time in testing out my social disability theory on opiate addicts. This entailed the very slow-moving collection of data from street addicts in their natural settings, work that was underfunded and often funded late as well. The turnaround time for journal submissions can be three to six months, and after each rejection one must revise the article to a new journal's format while attempting to forestall in the future the complaints raised by the last set of referees. As one thus attempts to anticipate misunderstandings, the article grows longer, and soon referees and editors begin to complain of its length as well. All of this can be disastrous to an untenured person, as I was at that time.

The journal referee reports did not denounce my racial data explicitly. Instead, they betrayed signs of annoyance, misunderstanding, and impatience. Indeed, those reports are difficult to distinguish from the frequently frustrating and obtuse ones we have all encountered in connection with less controversial submissions. However, the data were good, the analysis was fairly straightforward, and the results were superior to anything then in existence. Yet, time and again the referee reports quibbled over definitions, elevated petty complaints to overriding importance, and conjectured in a paranoid way about the quality of the data instead of seeing them as social facts in their own right, whatever the final explanation of the substantial racial differentials they revealed in delinquency rates. An occasionally obtuse referee's report is part of anyone's fate, but when the same paper elicits such reactions several times, more than the luck of the draw is involved. As we shall see, this trend ceased abruptly when I submitted my papers outside the main sociological and criminological arena to journals in which the referees would be even more critical of methodology than average. The negativism toward the papers was, of course, bolstered by the awareness of the referees that official statistics had often been impugned by self-report studies—but not so thoroughly impugned, apparently, that they felt it safe to allow some official statistics to be presented in print as a basis for further discussion.

One could attempt to dignify the reactions of these journal referees by ascribing their behavior to the effects of operating under a dominant Kuhnian paradigm. However, all scientists are aware of the possibility of their judgment being affected by such transitory aberrations, and most make a conscious effort to remain open-minded, as the norms dictate. I have myself approved self-report studies for publication because the method has standing within the discipline at the moment, and the proper place to deal with the issue is in public. Journal editors, above all, are expected to be statesmanlike in this regard, especially when an author who feels abused remonstrates with them. In this case, I could make no real headway with the editors whatever. As far as they were concerned, if I were the victim of poor judgment, I could submit to some other journal. The possibility that such "poor judgment" was systematic did not occur to the editors—or to me—until I had already accumulated multiple rejections. I openly confess, moreover, that the papers, from a literary intellectual's point of view, were boring. Essentially demographic in cast, they did not offer the editor the prospect of exciting controversy if they appeared in his journal, only of boring controversy.

In desperation, I decided to submit the articles to journals that were quantitatively oriented and whose editors were also quantitatively adept. This produced a change in the tone of referee reports, which now exhibited more respect for data even though they might contain distasteful findings. Indeed, one could sense, I think, a greater respect and concern precisely because the results might be disturbing and, hence, rarely reported. Moreover, the editors themselves felt competent to adjudicate any remaining disagreements between authors and referees, and the articles were published finally (Gordon, 1973; Gordon and Gleser, 1974). To me, it felt as though I were at last dealing with real scientists, persons who would allow some disturbing data a little breathing space instead of stifling them before they could receive exposure to other members of the discipline.

I describe these matters to show that science leads ineluctably to confrontations between established opinion and new evidence. My work on race-specific data did not spring from a change in the political climate, as is sometimes alleged glibly in the case of Jensen (see Dworkin, 1974; Piel, 1978; Harwood, 1979). Instead, it emerged in the natural course of a long, systematic program of successful research on genuine scientific problems. This is not necessarily the only legitimate way in which challenges to established conceptions may arise—some may require less preparation, as witnessed by the next stage in my narrative. My point is simply that successful restriction of conclusions drawn from rational inquiry and the results of dialogue with other scientists must inevitably impose major distortions on what passes for scientific knowledge.

As it turned out, my work on race-specific delinquency rates led to an even more controversial finding. Quite serendipitously, two of the race-specific delinquency rates generated in the course of my work on prevalence were numbers familiar to users of normal probability tables as being approximately one standard deviation apart in cumulative probability. These were the rates of juvenile court record delinquency for white males and black males in Philadelphia, which were about 17% and 50%, respectively. Since I was already aware from Jensen's highly publicized article (1969) that the mean IQs of blacks and whites were one white standard deviation apart, I recognized instantly that these two delinquency rates had the property I have since come to call "IQ-commensurability." That is, the difference in rates was commensurate with the difference in IQ.

The other three racial pairs of rates that I had generated did not involve familiar numbers, so it was impossible to tell at a glance whether they shared the same property. Eventually, I looked them up in tables and found that they were consistent with the IQ-commensurability of the first pair. These results were published in invited articles, where I had ample space and did not have to contend with referees (Gordon, 1975a; 1976).

Often, the space and referee problems interact. When one has a controversial subject, more evidence is usually demanded, especially if it is a complex subject, and this requires longer papers. Hence, the space limitations imposed by our journals tend to work against scientific challenges while simultaneously providing a convenient excuse for rejecting unwelcome views, either because they are "undeveloped" or because the paper containing them is "too long." For example, Jensen's (1969) best-known paper was the longest ever published in the journal in which it appeared, but it was also an invited one, so its length did not hinder its publication. An interesting example of the utility of "length" as a pretext for polite rejection can be found in a book by Podhoretz (1979: 205), which describes various aspects of the "terror" unleashed within the New York literary intellectual world against those who question radical leftist dogma. In this case, the *New York Review of Books* turned down an article it had previously solicited from Nathan Glazer when he failed to take a sufficiently positive view of radical student action at Berkeley, on the grounds that his paper was "too long."

The property of the delinquency rates that I call IQ-commensurability had not played any role in my earlier difficulties with journal referees because there was no point in my drawing attention to this property within the limited space of those prior papers. Because of this important lead that had developed from the data, however, I had been obliged to decline one editor's compromise offer to publish an extremely sketchy version of one of the earlier papers that would contain only the conclusions. Apparently, this editor felt compelled to make this gesture because the work we were correcting had appeared originally in his own journal. Such a compromise would have furnished too flimsy a foundation from which to face the controversy that I anticipated might follow my development of the IQ issue. Consequently, I continued submitting those early papers elsewhere until, as I described, they were accepted in highly quantitative journals.

Quite aside from the importance of the prevalence data for resolving the self-report problem—my original goal—the IQ-commensurability of the rates reinforced my conviction that the official data were probably meaningful in some deeper sense than mere description, for why else would such a lawful relation hold over four pairs of rates for two sexes and two widely different levels of severity of delinquency in different jurisdictions and at slightly different points in time? Unfortunately, I could not even allude to this important fact in the earlier papers for fear of making them even less attractive. Thus, we have another example of the perverse effects that research taboos can have on science even when the researcher in question does not subscribe himself to the taboo.

Because I chose to publish my lengthy work on IQ-commensurability as an invited article, I never did test the tolerance of our journals toward this idea. Hirschi and Hindelang (1977) eventually did succeed in reaching a journal audience at about the same time, but apparently only after encountering some frustrating delays. Their article concerned itself with IQ and delinquency too, but not very controversially with race.

Invited articles in books, or books themselves, if one has that much to say at any given moment, clearly play a vital role in maintaining intellectual freedom, especially when the editor of the book does not know in advance exactly what he is getting. Because I was able to put two such invitations back to back, I was able to deal first with the problem of the culture-fairness of IQ tests themselves (Gordon, 1975b), which I regarded as intellectually prior to my thesis concerning IQ and delinquency. Not having to deal with journals at that point made it possible to develop my ideas in an orderly manner without setbacks from rejections. But publication in books does not force material on the attention of a discipline to the same extent as publication in a major journal, and the book reviews that might compensate for this deficiency are notoriously unreliable (see, for example, the account of reviews of his book, *Making It,* in Podhoretz.

1979, and the review of Ornstein's *Race and Politics in School/ Community Organizations* by Jackson, 1977). One review (Coie, 1976) did not even mention the existence of my invited chapter dealing with IQ tests in the volume edited by Walter Gove (Gordon, 1975b)—out of politeness, one assumes—and another (Austin, 1977) gave no idea at all of the contents of my invited chapter on prevalence, IQ, and race in a volume edited by Malcolm Klein (Gordon, 1976), while alleging that it had "a number" of unspecified "defects." Sagarin and Montanino's review (1976) of the Gove volume was a refreshing exception to this tendency.

As one becomes concerned with this controversial topic, one acquires a deeper awareness of the frailties of many and the importance of integrity on the part of a few. Many of the unpleasant consequences of pursuing these and related scientific matters have been detailed by Jensen (1972: 1-67) and Herrnstein (1973: 3-59). The latter's analysis of the poor showing that our academic establishment makes in supporting free expression is especially penetrating. The penalties for dissenting from the orthodoxy of the intellectual establishment across a broader front have been treated by Podhoretz (1979) in a book that is probably the most important account of the behavior of literary intellectuals ever to appear. Not all of the nasty details are publicly revealed in these works, I know for a fact, but that need not matter for our present purposes.

I myself have experienced a few disadvantages that I can identify with some confidence, including the loss of a job opportunity that would have added at least $100,000 to my lifetime earnings. On the whole, however, I have been fortunate, because Johns Hopkins is a small university where many faculty members knew me personally before my research interests became controversial and where the usual proportion of radicals is too few in absolute numbers to achieve critical mass. In fact, after the atmosphere of the 1960s, intellectual life on campus seems now to be almost idyllic, particularly when one has tenure.

Throughout the recent past, at least a few scientists have performed their roles in strict accordance with scientific ideals, as witnessed by the appearance in refereed journals of numerous articles by Jensen, his election as a Fellow of the American Association for the Advancement of Science despite strenuous objections from Margaret Mead and others (Boffey, 1977), and his long overdue promotion to a distinguished rank at Berkeley despite opposition from colleagues in the "humanistic foundations" within his own School of Education. Indeed, psychology appears to have functioned reasonably well as a science during this extremely troubled time, thanks to a few. I am reminded by this of the legend of the *Lamed-Vov,* the 36 "hidden saints" in ordinary walks of life upon whom, according to Hasidic tradition, the continued existence of the world depends at any given time (Singer, 1965: 80). Individual decency and courage count far more heavily than usual at precisely such times, and anyone who doubts that he can have an effect is seriously mistaken.

To my surprise (again, thanks to a few), modern science as an institution does really provide compensating opportunities to those who challenge orthodox views. Witness the fact that I was invited to speak before the American Society of Criminology by C. Ray Jeffery last year and by Edward Sagarin this year and that I have an invitation to present a paper at the American Sociological Association convention next year. These opportunities offset to some extent the disadvantages of reduced exposure caused by having to turn from journals to alternative forms of publication.

Painting too rosy a picture, however, would be a mistake. Perhaps I an unnecessarily pessimistic, but I do not, for example, risk wasting my time by applying for federal funds. Just a few individuals in influential positions are sufficient to veto support, and if they are sophisticated enough they can sabotage decisions without seeming to depart from universalistic criteria. Consequently, I fund my research out of my own pocket. Wherever hiring or funding is decided by a committee—and that is the usual practice—one is vulnerable, because enforcers of taboos on topics are numerous, and just a few strong objections can be decisive in highly competitive situations. Although such behavior is transparently unethical and, conceivably, illegal, some individuals apparently find it expedient to assert that this is actually the moral thing.

In his chapter in this book, Karmen claims that taboos do not exist and are not operative in contemporary social science. He asserts that opposition to ideas linking race and IQ is mainly aboveboard and part of normal scientific fair play, and that complaints of interference are but a tactic for enlisting support for views otherwise questionable on scientific grounds. It is certainly not evident to me that Karmen has established a convincing basis for drawing this conclusion. His own mentor, Sagarin, whom Karmen questions for support in other places, stated in his book review that my citations of Jensen's work would place me "on target" for ad hominem polemicists (Sagarin and Montanino, 1976: 262). Letters I have written to influential periodicals such as the *New York Times* (the editorial opinion page of which is heavily committed to the New Left, according to Podhoretz, 1979: 306) and *Scientific American* (whose publisher's views can be sampled in Piel, 1978) in response to unfair and inaccurate articles on race and IQ are never printed. Others have told me of having the same experience (see also Jensen, 1972: 17-21). Consequently, Jensen and others are made to appear more isolated than the facts warrant. I and others have also noted younger colleagues skirting controversial issues for fear of not receiving research funds or of otherwise damaging their careers. Senior colleagues often express what appears to be sincere agreement on many of these issues in private, but point out that it is foolhardy to take a position publicly (for similar cases, see Jensen, 1972: 46-47). Then, too, there are the demonstrations that have prevented Jensen, Herrnstein, and Shockley from speaking on many campuses (e.g., Minnesota Daily, 1976; Thompson, 1978; Herrnstein, 1973: 30-41; Jensen, 1972: 47-48; Goodell, 1977: 200) and the physical attack on Eysenck at the London School of Economics (Izbicki, 1973). In 1972, James Q. Wilson said of Harvard, "the list of subjects that cannot be publicly discussed there in a free and open forum has grown steadily," and he specifically included policy concerning blacks and the relationship between intelligence and heredity among his several examples (quoted in Podhoretz, 1979: 328). If these are not symptoms of a taboo, what are they?

In his Chart 1, Karmen presents specimen quotations intended to demonstrate that the principle of free scientific inquiry has been upheld consistently by professional organizations and that it is only the scientific basis of arguments by Jensen and others with which such organizations have found fault. Let us consider only the last four passages in Karmen's chart, since these are the only ones having any connection to Jensen and recent events. Karmen maintains that these passages "criticize irresponsible statements and refute falsifications," but the irresponsible statements in question are not Jensen's, and no falsifications are refuted, since no scientific evidence appears in the passages.

The first of Karmen's last three quoted passages was revived as part of a resolution that the American Anthropological Association sent to all of its members after the publication of Jensen's 1969 article. Although Jensen never suggested that the exclusion of any race from rights guaranteed by the Constitution was justified on any basis or that any race was totally lacking in any ability, let alone abilities "needed to participate fully in the democratic way of life and in modern technological civilization" (as the original passage goes on to state in sections omitted by Karmen), the AAA resolution solemnly continued: "And whereas a recent article . . . by Arthur R. Jensen . . . cast doubt on this conclusion." Apparently, this malicious distortion of Jensen's article meets Karmen's standards of fair play, freedom of scientific inquiry, and refutation of evidence. (For the full text of the AAA resolution and further discussion, see Jensen, 1972: 37-39.) The second passage can be passed over for a moment.

The third of Karmen's last four passages comes from a lengthy statement issued by the Council of the Society for the Psychological Study of Social Issues that consisted in part of a word-for-word revival of an earlier criticism directed at someone else in 1961. As Jensen (1972: 37) later wrote, "this simple pigeon-holing operation on the part of the SPSSI Council might at least partially explain their illfitting and misleading 'criticism' of my . . . article." One of the signers of the SPSSI statement later apologized to Jensen for letting his name be used in that way (see Jensen, 1972: 32-43).

The last of Karmen's passages comes from a motion passed unanimously by the Council of the American Anthropological Association (Newsletter of the AAA, 1972: 12). Astute readers will note the gratuitous and reflex-like insertion of the word "sexist" in this 1971 resolution and correctly interpret its inclusion as indicative of the deliberation given by the anthropologists to the remaining substance of their motion. Although this 1971 AAA motion "condemns as dangerous and unscientific the racist, sexist or anti-working class [sic] theories of genetic inferiority propagated by R. Herrnstein, W. Shockley and A. Jensen," the only material bearing on sexual differences by any of these writers at that time was an obscure article by Jensen (1971) published in a book during the same year the motion was passed. Most probably, members of the unanimously voting AAA Council had never even heard of this paper by Jensen, let alone read it, but had they done so they would have discovered that the paper summarized results from numerous cognitive ability tests and reported that the "overall weighted mean sex difference favors females" (Jensen, 1971: 144).

Now let us return to the second of the last four passages, which I temporarily skipped over. Unlike the other recent ones in Karmen's chart, this passage from the National Academy of Sciences does not originate from an organization of social scientists, but rather from an organization composed mainly of eminent natural scientists. It stands out from the rest in being much more encouraging toward research on genetic hypotheses and in stressing the ambiguous nature of existing evidence concerning racial differences. Consequently, it is the exception that proves the rule—if all statements were like the one from the NAS, I would be inclined to say there was no taboo.

In contrast, the later-revived 1961 AAA statement repudiates as an unwarranted conclusion what was offered only as a hypothesis by Jensen and Shockley; the 1969 SPSSI statement denounces heritability estimates within race despite the fact that evidence of substantial genetic control over IQ is not at all ambiguous (witness the seven-point absolute difference between identical twins reared apart, excluding Burt's data, versus the eleven-point or greater difference between sibs and fraternal twins reared together); and the 1971 AAA statement condemns everything, including theories. By acknowledging the ambiguity in the evidence concerning racial differences, the NAS statement implicitly asserts that it is by no means clear that the difference in IQ is determined environmentally, which is essentially the point made by Jensen and Shockley.

When one is challenging entrenched views, it is sometimes difficult to distinguish malicious prejudice from run-of-the-mill scientific bad judgment. An example of the latter will put the former in perspective. Some years ago, just after sharing the AAAS Socio-Psychological Prize (for 1974) for a paper on opiate addiction that had also encountered stubborn resistance from referees who preferred dealing with controversy behind the scenes, I tried to cash in on my momentary celebrity by requesting federal support that would enable me to continue my work on both the self-report problem and opiate addiction under a single financial umbrella. I realized at the time that it was my last opportunity to obtain funds before the more controversial aspects of my work became known. But my proposal was turned down on the recommendation of outside reviewers, who supposedly said that "a methodological examination of the self-report literature, even by a researcher of your competence, was not likely to settle the issue." As far as I was concerned, I had the problem already solved.

I needed that support so that I could work on several seemingly unrelated topics that would all qualify as evidence of progress on a single grant. When pursuing complex and controversial matters, it is often necessary to follow the trail into strange fields, respond to opponents who raise unexpected issues, criticize targets of opportunity, and learn about new areas. I had found out while working on opiate addiction that a normal grant can serve as a straitjacket for someone who needs flexibility in pursuing new leads. Science is not business. During the period in which my drug grant ran, I worked hard to turn my research orientation toward IQ, which by then I had recognized to be a most crucial variable in need of urgent attention, but this work could not count toward fulfilling the requirements of the grant. Exhausted by working on too many different things, most of which would not satisfy the granting agency,

I felt like a borrower who needs to consolidate his debts. As far as I am concerned, the rejection of my umbrella proposal at that time was as damaging to my research and career as the tactics of those who would suppress research on what they define as taboo topics. This illustrates that determining whether a professional evaluation is seriously biased or merely seriously mistaken is often impossible. In this case, if what I regarded to be a singularly poor research-funding decision had come after the more controversial aspects of my work were publicly apparent, I would have found it hard not to entertain paranoid conjectures. Once set loose within an intellectual community, the burden of such paranoia when added to the normal insecurities of creative work can be incredibly discouraging and demoralizing, as witnessed by the signs of fatigue, failure of nerve, and just plain knuckling under exhibited even by some of the most formidable members of the New York literary intellectual community in the face of the "terror," as Podhoretz (1979) calls it, fostered by the New Left in its heyday.

PERSONAL ORIGINS OF MY RECENT RESEARCH: THE AD HOMINEM APPROACH AND SURROUNDING ISSUES

According to Marxist sociologists of knowledge, the most relevant factor for me to confess is my social class background. It is often alleged that scientists simply try to confirm their individual biases and that these biases are established by their class backgrounds or present self-interest. Of course, "bias" in this context is an equivocal word that robs even correct positions of the respect due them. Our science seems rife with these corrosive terminologies nowadays.

As a trained scientist and rather introspective person, I have tried to play the sociology-of-knowledge game to see what it would yield, in contrast to the account I have given in the preceding section. There is no point in going into details. Let it suffice to say that I could easily go on to write my autobiography, like some poor prisoner being "brainwashed." As we delved ever deeper into my past life, as with anyone's life, we would turn up a mixed bag of material. Social class suggests this, later childhood suggests that, and so we would go, zigging and zagging through my past, the final impression depending on where we chose to stop and on what weights we arbitrarily assigned to the various elements in summing up the whole. Meanwhile, everyone except perhaps a few in the audience would have become distracted from the scientific issues, as we all become increasingly absorbed in what was tacitly being acknowledged as a relevant area of scientific concern.

Even if I emerged untarnished from such scrutiny after all our labors, this would not add one whit to the correctness of facts or the plausibility of interpretations in my scientific work, which could still be totally wrong! By the same reasoning, unless we adopt a double-standard, no amount of personally damaging material ought to impugn the quality of my science, which should stand or fall on its own merits. What is not sauce for the goose ought not to be sauce for the gander, and if the personal area of inquiry is doomed to be irrelevant therefore, why waste time on it in the first place?

Used in this way, the sociology of knowledge is essentially an ad hominem argument dressed up in pseudoscientific garb. Nevertheless, I have often wondered if essentially ad hominem arguments serve any useful purpose in science. Most of us, including myself, want to know more about other scientists, apparently as an aid in identifying their overall orientation and in judging their credibility for purposes of initial screening. Used in this way, I suppose, personal information can serve as a useful sensitizing device, but it is never a substitute for or even a supplement to the serious conduct of scientific argument. I myself would never think of disposing publicly of an opponent's argument by dismissing him, say, as a "Marxist," even if I felt this to be justified. All too often, sociologists of knowledge try to capitalize on the sensitizing function of personal information in an attempt to convince us that such information can substitute for scientific knowledge in resolving controversy. This simply does not work, not even insofar as credibility is concerned, because having been right or wrong yesterday is no guarantee that one is right or wrong today. The sensitizing function can serve as a time-saving device for allocating attention on a day-to-day basis, but once a serious controversy has broken out, and the time-saving function has been corrupted by mud-slinging and epithets, we have no alternative but to dig into the scientific evidence and see for ourselves.

In light of these remarks, I would like to consider two labels that are often applied to protagonists on either side of these taboo issues—"racist" and "Marxist" (or, more generally, "leftist"). "Racist" is probably the most intimidating label of all to intellectuals, with the single exception of "anti-Semite." Independently, Podhoretz (1979: 141) reaches a similar conclusion, placing "racist" second only to "Nazi" in offensiveness. Fear of being even unjustly accused of "racism" inhibits many intellectuals from speaking their minds on currently important topics, and there is no doubt the epithet is applied freely nowadays. But what does it mean?

Two possibilities suggest themselves. According to one (a rather archaic usage, incidentally), a racist is someone who entertains the possibility that there is a nontrivial difference, perhaps genetic in origin, between racial groups in some important characteristic. Clearly, if a scientist reports or hypothesizes such a difference, we have added nothing to the content of discourse by describing him in addition as a "racist." Employed in this way, the term is simply redundant. Certainly, it does not tell us whether his observation or hypothesis is right or wrong. If this is all there is to the word, why should it be so intimidating? Such ideas might be unpopular, but they are hardly intrinsically immoral.

But "racist" is used in a second sense, to describe individuals who do not differentiate between members within a racial category, and who hold toward them as a category positive or negative attitudes in excess of what facts warrant. In this sense, use of the term "racist" conveys something in addition to the first sense that is not easily communicated by other means, something plainly unscientific and gratuitously invidious.

I suspect that it is the ease of confusing these two senses that renders the term such a terrifying epithet to intellectuals. Usually, whether the second sense applied to a scientist whose work qualified him for the first sense would be difficult to determine, but the term can easily be made to do double duty as a smear simply because of its ambiguity. Since the first sense adds no new meaning whatever, it strikes me as unfair to ignore and unprincipled to exploit the ambiguity of this term by using it in the first sense only, when it can so easily be mistaken for the second sense. Before using the term, therefore, persons should be prepared to go on record that they do intend it in the second sense, since that is the only one that adds anything new to the discourse. Presumably, when used accurately in this second sense to describe a scientist, "racist" would serve at least in a sensitizing role. It would still not tell us whether a person's science is right or wrong. No ad hominem argument can accomplish that. But at least it would represent an improvement over the inaccurate or ambiguous use of the word, when it serves merely as a bludgeon for bullying opponents (see, for example, the author's reaction to being called a racist by Stokely Carmichael in Podhoretz, 1979: 141).

The labels "Marxist" and "leftist" are not especially threatening epithets in contemporary academia, but they do have content and thus perform a sensitizing function. For our present purposes, we need only be concerned with leftists who claim to have respect for scientific evidence, thus ignoring an issue with respect to a small minority of leftists that recently aroused protest within British academic circles when the question of their scientific integrity was raised (Scott, 1977; Scully, 1977).

Surveys reported in 1972 indicated that the social sciences were more left of center politically than any other discipline, and that among the social sciences sociology was the most left of all (Ladd and Lipset, 1972: Table 1; Lipset and Ladd, 1972: Tables 1 and 2). Although recently the humanities seem to have caught up (Ladd and Lipset, 1978; for a possible explanation, see Podhoretz, 1979), these facts lead to one of two conclusions. Either social scientists know something about the world that other academic intellectuals do not (but which persons in the humanities have also recently discovered, despite apparent differences in method and substance between the fields) or there is something peculiar about their outlook. Even a modicum of modesty ought to lead leftists to serious consideration of the second possibility. After all, we are not talking about expertise only in some narrow specialized area, but of an entire world view that conditions scientific positions down to the details of highly technical matters across a broad array of issues, particularly with respect to what views are opposed.

Impeccable standards of fairness are always important to any discipline that contains so many of a single persuasion. Otherwise, the credibility of the discipline in the eye of the public may be damaged beyond repair. Quoting Sprehe (1967) directly, Lipset and Ladd (1972: 75) drew attention to the fact that "the more research funds a respondent is responsible for, the more likely he was to score low on Value Freeness" in sociological research, and that "radicalism tended to increase . . . as the amount of research funds grew larger, except for the very highest category." If sociologists were to discover such correlations between analogous variables in other sectors of society such as business or politics, they would probably suspect that something was rotten in Denmark and be quite vocal about it. Only a widespread conviction among sociologists that they already had the answers would suffice to blunt the implications of Sprehe's findings concerning the integrity of their own discipline. But such a conviction is the most unscientific attitude of all.

In science, new knowledge is sometimes resisted in excess of what the norms would indicate. The statistician Fisher (Box, 1978: 131), for example, put it well:

> A scientific career is peculiar in some ways. Its *raison d'être* is the increase of natural knowledge. Occasionally, therefore, an increase of natural knowledge occurs. But this is tactless, and feelings are hurt. For in some small degree it is inevitable that views previously expounded are shown to be either obsolete or false. Most people, I think, can recognize this and take it in good part if what they have been teaching for ten years or so comes to need a little revision; but some undoubtedly take it hard as a blow to their *amour propre*, or even as an invasion of the territory they had come to think of as exclusively their own, and they must react with . . . ferocity.

In social science, however, where entire world views may be at stake, ideology interacts with normal amour propre to produce a much stronger emotional antagonism to unorthodox ideas than would be expected in statistics.

Thus, we get such catchy phrases as the oft-quoted "blaming the victim" (Ryan, 1971), which dismisses entire categories of research in three words. Anyone who reports unflattering data about the disadvantaged who does not immediately link the data to a denunciation of our capitalist society, our racist society, or the social class structure—in short, who cannot find any acceptable place to dump what some of our most verbally fluent intellectuals can only conceive of as "the blame"—is guilty of blaming the victim. Looking back, it suddenly becomes clear why my social disability thesis has been unpopular; why the finding—laughed at on the street because it is so obvious—that long-term heroin addicts receive pleasure from their drug was first rejected despite overwhelming evidence (McAuliffe and Gordon, 1974; 1975); why the unequivocal evidence that IQ differences between blacks and whites are real is successfully ignored by Mercer (Gordon, 1975b; Gordon and Rudert, 1979); why one cannot publish race-specific delinquency rates easily; why the relation between IQ and delinquency is so unwelcome; why Moynihan was vilified for giving too accurate a picture of black family life even though he showed much concern (Rainwater and Yancey, 1967); why Jensen is seldom read and often denounced. All of these can be interpreted as instances of blaming the victim.

The assumption is, apparently, that we already know who is the victim and who is the victimizer. With these issues decided in advance, science itself becomes taboo. But if there has been a systematic mistake, then the victimizer must be the social scientist who forecloses debate, because without correct diagnosis there is seldom a solution. As misdiagnosed problems worsen, sooner or later we all become victims (see, for example, the issue of Ebony, August 1979, devoted to black-on-black crime).

CLOSE EXAMINATION OF A MAJOR DISTRACTOR IN THE IQ DEBATE

There are a number of rhetorical devices and classic fallacies of the ad hominem and ad populum varieties that we see again and again in debate concerning IQ. These function like powerful distractors in multiple choice questions; they look plausible while diverting attention from the right answers. The word "inferiority," which connotes a global qualitative difference applicable to all members of a category, is a favorite choice of journalists, for example, when referring to issues involving mean differences and considerable dispersion of individual scores on a particular variable. Adolf Hitler puts in a frequent appearance too, somewhat ironically, because there are more references to his name than to that of any other person in a well-known book concerned with fallacies in argument (Fearnside and Holther, 1959). Not only was Hitler himself a master of fallacy, but his name is now often used as the central stimulus in classic examples of fallacious reasoning.

Most of these devices are transparent to thoughtful persons, but there is one that disturbs even these, and that is the one that raises the specter of genocide. Even veiled allusions to the Jewish Holocaust, which the mere mention of Hitler always evokes, but which are often introduced in their own right, raise serious doubts in some people's minds as to whether research on IQ should be permitted. People object not only because the research might prove to be mistaken, but also because it might prove to be correct and somehow lead to genocide in either case.

I am not referring now simply to the more flamboyant uses of the word "genocide" by the press and by demagogues in situations where it is not even remotely appropriate, as in connection with birth control (see, for example, the sensible discussion by Weisbord, 1975), but to the real thing.

If there is conceivably a field of research that might legitimately be declared taboo, I would think one that had a serious probability of leading to genocide would come as close as any. Let us, therefore, take an honest look at the possibility that research on IQ differences might produce genocide, instead of using the issue as an unanalyzed rhetorical device.

How serious the probability is depends on the scenario that one chooses for connecting remote events. According to the scenario commonly implied, the linkage is established with the same facility one observes on a popular TV program about science, in which, "by tracing a single thread up through what is in reality a pyramid of developments leading up to one particular invention, a false sense of cause and effect is often introduced"; consequently, the program routinely promotes impressions such as, "if only Otto Guericke hadn't demonstrated his vacuum to Emperor Ferdinand in 1654, the atom bomb wouldn't have been invented" (Chedd, 1979: 102). In similar fashion, the usual scenario would have us believe that IQ research and genocide are practically synonymous, and that there would not be a complex web of intervening and alternative possibilities even if these two events were to have some tenuous, remote connection.

Shockley (1972: 17) attempted to inject some realism into the discussion of genocide by pointing out that a working First Amendment—and, hence, a free press in Germany—would have prevented the terrible fate of the Jews. While this suggestion is an improvement, it seems to accept the underlying premise while depending on only one factor, albeit an important one, for avoiding genocide.

A still more balanced perspective can be achieved if we realize that there are many other genocide scenarios one might propose, and that in some of these the concealment of genuine IQ differences could lead to tragedy. It is well-established that people can estimate relative intelligence fairly well without IQ measurements. Attempting to conceal differences could eventually discredit rational authority, squander valuable lead-time better spent working on solutions, and leave matters to political demogogues by default as a complex social situation progressively deteriorated. Populations responsible for genocide in the past have not waited for scientists. Those seriously concerned about genocide have an obligation to weigh all of the alternative scenarios, not just those that yield them the maximum rhetorical advantage.

The central assumption in the usual genocide allusion is that lower IQ (whether real or imagined) somehow places a population at greater risk. Let us turn, for a change, to the empirical facts, which so often provide new insight into old assumptions. To test this assumption, I have examined as many instances of genuine genocide occurring in this century as I could clearly identify in a brief time, to see who were the victims and who the victimizers.

Let us start with the Jewish Holocaust, since that is the case that is foremost in everyone's mind. At about 113, the mean verbal IQ of Jews of European descent is the highest of any known ethnic group (Gordon and Rudert, 1979: 182). The outstanding success of Jews measured according to all usual criteria is a widely recognized reflection of this statistic (Patai, 1977: chapters 11-14; Bermant, 1977; Goldberg, 1976). On the other hand, there is no reason to suppose that the IQ of the Germans departed appreciably from the general white average of 100. In fact, if one peruses Hitler's *Mein Kampf* (1939: 75-83), one finds that the prominence of Jews in the intellectual life of Vienna played a role in his anti-Semitism, and that he recognized their intellect (1939: 412, 416) even while he fulminated against them. So here we have genocide committed against a higher IQ population by members of a lower IQ population.

The evidence concerning the 600,000 or more Armenians (virtually one out of three) who died during their genocidal persecution in Turkey in 1915 reveals the same pattern. The Armenians were widely considered to be intellectually more able and more industrious than the Turks, whose genius supposedly lay in military matters (Toynbee, 1915: 18-19, 112-116; El-Ghusein, 1918: 11-13, 50; Niepage, 1917: 20-21; Morgenthau, 1974: 6-8, 12, 66, 74; Boyajian, 1972: 14, 29-30, 306-307, 358-359, 402-403; Baliozian, 1975: 121-131). Reflecting this general appraisal in his sympathetic novel, Werfel (1934: 83, 338) described Armenians as "a race of merchants and craftsman . . . of bookworms" and "of puny intellectuals" and depicted Turks as warriors. The prosperity of Armenians in our country would seem to bear out these impressions. However, novelist Werfel's stereotype of intellectuals overlooked the fact that Armenians—like modern Israelis—could prove themselves capable warriors when circumstances warranted (Boyajian, 1972: 79, 106; Baliozian, 1975: 166; Morgenthau, 1974: 12, 28). Armenian intellectuals were apt to be special targets of arrest or execution (Boyajian, 1972: 150; Mugerditchian, n.d.: 5-10). Morgenthau (1974: 40) reported, "The gendarmes showed a particular desire to annihilate the educated and the influential."

Because of their intelligence, educational achievements, and prominence in public life, the Ibos of Nigeria were often likened to the Jews (Garrison, 1967; Bourjaily, 1970). At least partly because of these qualities, 30,000 were killed in pogroms, and another two million died in the ensuing war.

The internecine strife between the Hutu and Tutsi in Burundi resulted at one point in the selective slaughter of some "80,000 educated" Hutu tribesmen (New York Times, 1973).

In Uganda, under Amin, "prominent Christians, intellectuals, well-to-do businessmen and people with political pasts as well as their relatives" were targets for elimination "regardless of their tribal origins" (Kaufman, 1977). Amin's army was said to consist of uneducated officers and thieves from the streets (Evening Sun, 1979a) who later went on killing rampages against ordinary citizens (Evening Sun, 1979b, 1979c; see also New York Times, 1977).

During a reign of terror in Ethiopia, secondary-school students were often dragged away in the middle of the night for execution (Darnton, 1978). In Equatorial Guinea, we learn that "a Cameroonian diplomat who recently ended a two-year assignment in Malabo said President Masie seemed to be intent on wiping out all political leaders, high government officials, professional men, businessmen and intellectuals who do not belong to his immediate tribal group" (New York Times, 1978). Thousands were reported to have died. Emperor Bokassa I of the Central African Empire (now Republic) personally took part in the massacre of schoolchildren and students, some of whom had rebelled against having to purchase uniforms from a company controlled by one of his wives (New York Times, 1979a, 1979b), but here the number killed was only about 100. Perhaps this one example does not qualify as genocide, but it fits in with the trend; once again, individuals were being killed for what they were, not for what they did.

Reports from Bangladesh during its struggle for independence stated that "the Pakistani authorities had begun a campaign to eliminate university professors and students and indeed all of the region's intellectual elite" (New York Times, 1971: 2). "On orders, the army—now consisting entirely of West Pakistani troops—has killed students, intellectuals, professors, engineers, doctors and others of leadership caliber—whether they were directly involved with the nationalist movement or not. An engineer . . . left because 'it was systematic killing of the educated. If I had stayed,' he said softly, 'It would have meant death, certainly death' " (Schanberg, 1971a: 12; see also 1971b).

During the genocide practiced against the urban population of Cambodia (most educated Cambodians lived in Phnom Penh) by a largely rural peasant revolutionary army (see Kamm, 1979: A8), "the principal targets for extermination, according to all accounts, continue to be former government employees, soldiers and those in Cambodia called 'intellectuals,' those with higher education. A devastating new element that emerges from the refugees' accounts . . . is that the regime now appears to be methodically killing wives and children, many long after the husbands were killed" (The Sun, 1978: A12).

> Intellectuals were systematically purged. . . . Survivors reported that all people who were known to speak foreign languages were hunted down, imprisoned and, in some cases, beaten to death with sticks. One doctor told the relief officials he had decided to hide his eyeglasses during the four years of Mr. Pol Pot's rule for fear of being revealed as an intellectual, and punished.

> Of more than 500 doctors known to have been practicing medicine in Cambodia . . . only 40 have been found. The rest are presumed to have been slain or to have died while working in the fields in the last four years.

> The first-hand evidence of torture was found at a former French high school in Phnom Penh that had been converted to a political prison, the official said, "and there were 5,000 files in the prison" [Hersh, 1979: A8].

Another Cambodian report stated, "Those who have more than a 7th grade education are condemned as 'the dandruff of society' " (Meyer, 1978). An official estimated that 85% to 90% of Cambodia's intellectuals were killed (Kamm, 1979: A8).

Whatever gave anyone the idea that a group's lower IQ placed them at special risk of genocide? Certainly, many individuals of all IQs died in these terrible persecutions, but there is clearly a pronounced bias guaranteeing that the average IQ of the victims was higher than that of the survivors or victimizers. Only the case of the Nazi genocide against Gypsies seems unclassifiable at this time.

Some may question the inclusion of intellectual strata along with ethnic populations in examples of genocide, but a little thought should dispel the notion that this artificially con- tributes to the overall picture. First of all, the intellectuals, like the Jews, were being eradicated because of who they were and not because of what they did. This has been a key feature for Jews in defining the Holocaust as an extraordinary form of mass killing (Wiesel, 1979: 38-39). Second, because of assortative mating, intellectuals always constitute a population that is somewhat distinct genetically (see Herrnstein, 1973), as well as distinct in beliefs. Greeley (1970), for example, has called attention to numerous similarities between intellectuals as a group and ethnic groups proper. Third, if one reads *Mein Kampf* critically, one can easily recognize it as an anti-intellectual diatribe, although this aspect of the work is generally obscured in commentaries of the time because of concern—justifiable in light of the material I have just reviewed—that any recognition of the intellectuality of the Jews would only serve to fan antagonism toward them. Consequently, our most classic and best-documented specimen of genocide is also one that upholds in detail the general thesis that emerges from this historical review, for in this case we have some insight into the personal motives behind the policy.

CONCLUSION

I do not recognize research on IQ, race, and delinquency—or, for that matter, on any other topic—as taboo. I have reviewed how I came to be concerned with this topic, and I have contrasted it with the ad hominem explanation fostered by those who set themselves up as authorities on what others are allowed to know. I have also examined the major rhetorical devices employed by those who wish to enforce taboos in science, and I have illustrated, by giving the problem of genocide serious consideration, that these devices do not reflect a genuine scholarly concern with substantive issues. I have also called attention in a modest way to certain disadvantages incurred by those who attempt to investigate what others designate as taboo topics, as well as some offsetting advantages. It remains to be seen to what extent our social sciences will continue to tolerate the tax on reason that these disadvantages represent. If "the power to tax is the power to destroy," and in the final analysis reason is our only hope, how much of this can our society afford before it too is destroyed?

REFERENCES

American Anthropological Association (1972) "Motions." Newsletter 13: 12.

AUSTIN, R. L. (1977) Survey review of "The Juvenile Justice System," ed. by M. W. Klein. Contemporary Sociology 6: 430-432.

BALIOZIAN, A. (1975) The Armenians: Their History and Culture. Toronto: Kar Publishing.

BERMANT, C. (1977) The Jews. New York: Times Books.

BOFFEY, P. M. (1977) "Dispute over Jensen election as Fellow flares in council." Science 195: 965.

BOURJAILY, V. (1970) "An epitaph for Biafra." New York Times Magazine (January 25): p. 32ff.

BOX, J. F. (1978) R. A. Fisher: The Life of a Scientist. New York: John Wiley.

BOYAJIAN, D. H. (1972) Armenia: The Case for a Forgotten Genocide. Westwood, NJ: Educational Book Crafters.

CHEDD, G. (1979) "Review of 'Connections,' PBS Television, Sunday evenings, September 30 through December 2." Science 80, 1: 102, 104.

COIE, J. D. (1976) Review of "The Labelling of Deviance: Evaluating a Perspective," ed. by W. R. Gove. Contemporary Psychology 21: 807-809.

DARNTON, J. (1978) "Ethiopia uses terror to control capital." New York Times (February 19): A1.

DWORKIN, G. (1974) "Two views on IQ." Amer. Psychologist 29: 465-468.

Ebony (1979) "Black-on-black crime." Vol. 34 (August).

EL-GHUSEIN, F. (1918) Martyred Armenia. New York: George H. Doran.

Evening Sun (Baltimore) (1979a) "Amin's secret police files reveal a prophetic letter." April 16: A4.

——— (1979b) "Amin troops reported on killing rampage." April 18: A2.

——— (1979c) "Amin troops reportedly slay 50." May 9: A3.

FEARNSIDE, W. W. and W. B. HOLTHER (1959) Fallacy: The Counterfeit of Argument. Englewood Cliffs, NJ: Prentice-Hall.

GARRISON, L. (1967) "The Ibos go it alone." New York Times Magazine (June 11): p. 30ff.

GOLDBERG, M. H. (1976) The Jewish Connection. New York: Stein and Day.

GOODELL, R. (1977) The Visible Scientist. Boston: Little Brown.

GORDON, R. A. (1963) Values and Gang Delinquency. Ph.D. dissertation, University of Chicago.

――― (1967a) "Social level, social disability, and gang interaction." Amer. J. of Sociology 73: 42-62.

――― (1967b) "Issues in the ecological study of delinquency." Amer. Soc. Rev. 32: 927-944.

――― (1968a) "On the interpretation of oblique factors." Amer. Soc. Rev. 33: 601-620.

――― (1968b) "Issues in multiple regression." Amer. J. of Sociology 73: 592-616.

――― (1973) "An explicit estimation of the prevalence of commitment to a training school, to age 18, by race and sex." J. of the Amer. Stat. Assn. 68: 547-553.

――― (1975a) "Crime and cognition: an evolutionary perspective," pp. 1-55 in Proceedings of the II International Symposium on Criminology. São Paulo, Brazil: Oscar Freire Institute.

――― (1975b) "Examining labelling theory: the case of mental retardation," pp. 83-146 in W. R. Gove (ed.) The Labelling of Deviance: Evaluating a Perspective. Beverly Hills, CA: Sage Publications.

――― (1976) "Prevalence: the rare datum in delinquency measurement and its implications for the theory of delinquency," pp. 201-284 in M. W. Klein (ed.), The Juvenile Justice System. Beverly Hills, CA: Sage Publications.

――― and L. J. GLESER (1974) "The estimation of the prevalence of delinquency: two approaches and a correction of the literature." J. of Mathematical Sociology 3: 275-291.

GORDON, R. A. and E. E. RUDERT (1979) "Bad news concerning IQ tests." Sociology of Education 52: 174-190.

GREELEY, A. (1970) "Intellectuals as an 'ethnic group.' " New York Times Magazine (July 12): p. 22ff.

GREENE, M. H. (1974) Estimating the Prevalence of Heroin Use in a Community. Special Action Office Monograph Series A, No. 4. Washington, DC: Executive Office of the President, Special Action Office for Drug Abuse Prevention.

HARWOOD, J. (1979) "Heredity, environment, and the legitimation of social policy," pp. 231-251 in B. Barnes and S. Shapin (eds.) Natural Order: Historical Studies of Scientific Culture. Beverly Hills, CA: Sage Publications.

HERRNSTEIN, R. J. (1973) IQ in the Meritocracy. Boston: Little, Brown.

HERSH, S. M. (1979) "2.25 million Cambodians are said to face starvation." New York Times (August 8): A1, A8.

HIRSCHI, T. and M. J. HINDELANG (1977) "Intelligence and delinquency: a revisionist review." Amer. Soc. Rev. 42: 571-587.

HITLER, A. (1939) Mein Kampf. New York: Reynal and Hitchcock.

IZBICKI, J. (1973) " 'Race' professor beaten up at LSE." Daily Telegraph (London), (May 9): 1.

JACKSON, G. D. (1977) Review of "Race and Politics in School/Community Organizations," by A. C. Ornstein. Contemporary Psychology 22: 115-117.

JENSEN, A. R. (1969) "How much can we boost IQ and scholastic achievement?" Harvard Educ. Rev. 39: 1-123.

——— (1971) "The race X sex X ability interaction," pp. 107-161 in R. Cancro (ed.) Intelligence: Genetic and Environmental Influences. New York: Grune & Stratton.

——— (1972) Genetics and Education. New York: Harper & Row.

Kamm, H. (1979) "Rebirth of ghostly Phnom Penh is attended by hunger and pain." New York Times (November 14): A1, A8.

KAUFMAN, M. T. (1977) "Uganda refugees say atrocities continue." New York Times (April 10): 6.

LADD, E. C., Jr. and S. M. LIPSET (1972) "Politics of American natural scientists and engineers." Science 176: 1091-1100.

——— (1978) "Professors found to be liberal but not radical." Chronicle of Higher Education 15 (January 16): 9.

LANDER, B. (1954) Towards an Understanding of Juvenile Delinquency: A Study of 8,464 Cases of Juvenile Delinquency in Baltimore. New York: Columbia Univ. Press.

LAPOUSE, R. (1967) "Problems in studying the prevalence of psychiatric disorder." Amer. J. of Public Health 57: 947-954.

LEIGHTON, D., J. S. HARDING, D. B. MACKLIN, A. M. MACMILLAN, and A. H. LEIGHTON (1963) The Character of Danger: Psychiatric Symptoms in Selected Communities. The Stirling Country Study, Vol. III. New York: Basic Books.

LIPSET, S. M. and E. C. LADD, Jr. (1972) "The politics of American sociologists." Amer. J. of Sociology 78: 67-104.

McAULIFFE, W. E. and R. A. GORDON (1974) "A test of Lindesmith's theory of addiction: the frequency of euphoria among long-term addicts." Amer. J. of Sociology 79: 795-840.

——— (1975) "Issues in testing Lindesmith's theory." Amer. J. of Sociology 81: 154-163.

MEYER, C. (1978) "Communist Cambodia seen as worse than Nazi Germany." Evening Sun (Baltimore), (April 28): A15.

Minnesota Daily (Minneapolis-St. Paul) (1976) "Protest of speaker's 'racism' disrupts seminar appearance." May 7.

MORGENTHAU, H. (1974) The Murder of a Nation. New York: Armenian General Benevolent Union of America. (First published in 1918.)

MUGERDITCHIAN, E. (n.d.) From Turkish Toils: The Narrative of an Armenian Family's Escape. New York: George H. Doran.

New York Times (1971) "All Mujib's aids reported seized." April 8: 1, 2.

——— (1973) "Witnesses tell of horror in new Burundi slaughter." June 17: 8.

——— (1977) "Amin said to execute 4 professors who fought naming school for him." August 7: 3.

——— (1978) "Killing of thousands reported in Guinea." January 25: A5.

——— (1979a) "Africa commission says Bokassa had role in massacre of children." August 17: A8.

——— (1979b) "Survivors describe massacre in Bangui." September 30: 15.

NIEPAGE, M. (1917) The Horrors of Aleppo: Seen by a German Eyewitness. London: T. Fisher Unwin.

PATAI, R. (1977) The Jewish Mind. New York: Scribner.

PIEL, G. (1978) "Research for action." Educational Researcher 7: 8-12.

PODHORETZ, N. (1979) Breaking Ranks. New York: Harper & Row.

RAINWATER, L. and W. L. YANCEY. (1967) The Moynihan Report and the Politics of Controversy. Cambridge, MA: MIT Press.

REISS, A. J., Jr. (1975) "Inappropriate theories and inadequate methods as policy plagues: self-reported delinquency and the law," pp. 211-222 in N. J. Demerath, III, O. Larsen, and K. F. Schuessler (eds.) Social Policy and Sociology. New York: Academic.

RYAN, W. (1971) Blaming the Victim. New York: Vintage.

SAGARIN, E. and F. MONTANINO (1976) "Anthologies and readers on deviance." Contemporary Sociology 5: 259-267.

SCHANBERG, S. H. (1971a) "Bengalis form a cabinet as bloodshed goes on." New York Times (April 14): 1, 12.

——— (1971b) "Hours of terror for a trapped Bengali officer." New York Times (April 17): 3.

SCHUESSLER, K. F. and D. R. CRESSEY (1950) "Personality characteristics of criminals." Amer. J. of Sociology 55: 476-484.

SCOTT, P. (1977) "Many British academics profess a vague sort of Marxism." Chronicle of Higher Education 15 (September 6): 10.

SCULLY, M. G. (1977) "Marxist 'penetration' charged in British higher education." Chronicle of Higher Education 15 (October 17): 8.

SHOCKLEY, W. (1972) "The apple-of-God's-eye obsession." The Humanist 32: 16-17.

SINGER, I. B. (1965) "A major Din Torah." Commentary 40: 77-80.

SPREHE, J. T. (1967) The Climate of Opinion in Sociology: A Study of the Professional Value and Belief Systems of Sociologists. Ph.D. dissertation, Washington University, St. Louis.

The Sun (Baltimore) (1978) "Refugees from Cambodia say bloodletting, starvation are still the rule." May 14: A12.

THOMPSON, R. (1978) " 'Unflappable' Jensen defends research." Daily Californian (Berkeley), (February 3): 1.

TOYNBEE, A. J. (1915) Armenian Atrocities: The Murder of a Nation. London: Hodder and Stoughton.

WEISBORD, R. G. (1975) Genocide? Birth Control and the Black American. Westport, CT: Greenwood Press.

WERFEL, F. (1934) The Forty Days of Musa Dagh. New York: Random House.

WIESEL, E. (1979) "Pilgrimage to the country of night." New York Times Magazine (November 4): p. 36ff.

4

S. Deon Henson

Rutgers University

FEMALE AS TOTEM, FEMALE AS TABOO:
An Inquiry into the Freedom to Make Connections

Facing the umbrella theme of taboo subjects in ciminology we must ask ourselves whether there is some reluctance to look at the relationship between feminism and increased female crime and, if so, whether this reluctance amounts to an irrational—even superstitious—fear which serves to thwart research and fix narrow limits on what we permit ourselves to know. In short, then, the question is: "Is female crime a taboo topic?"

THE CONCEPT OF TABOO

Taken together, the criteria from the *Encyclopedia Britannica* and Freud's *Totem and Taboo* yield an adequate, standard definition of taboo. From the former, we learn that taboo refers to a nonrational or supernatural prohibition which can apply to persons, things, or actions. Its relevance in the present context is to the subject matter (things), to the inquiry itself (actions), and perhaps to persons (females, or more specifically, female offenders).

It is not necessary to the definition that the prohibition function nonrationally, only that the reasons generally given for the taboo are supernatural or nonrational.

Freud (1946: 26) provides additional criteria:

> The meaning of taboo branches off into two opposite directions. On the one hand it means to us sacred, consecrated. On the other hand it means uncanny, dangerous, forbidden and unclean.

Further, Freud (1946: 34) notes that the sources of taboo

> begin where the most primitive and at the same time the most enduring human impulses have their origin, namely, in the fear of the effect of demonic powers.

All human behavior is motivated and rewarded by feelings of control over the environment. Control and its intellectual soulmate, predictability, allow the human animal to negotiate a way safely and satisfactorily in a chaotic world (Becker, 1964). Beyond simply surviving, the fullness or richness of life depends upon the extent of management control that an individual has mastered. To the degree that the power to control eludes us, or that our world overwhelms us, we focus on whatever portion or aspect of the world we can control. Becker (1973) calls this "fetishizing the field."[1] This fetishization permits the necessary business of life to continue when the repertoire of responses to the demands of life is severely limited. A taboo is just such a ritualistic exercise in control.

To summarize, then, a taboo is characterized by awe and aversion, ritualistic control of either the environment or beliefs about the environment, and a nonrational defense of the aversion (although the taboo itself may or may not be functionally purposive).

TABOO AND FEMALE CRIMINALITY

Two things can be stated at the outset:

(1) The ordinary notion of taboo (as culled from these basic, standard sources) does not, without straining the definition beyond usefulness, accommodate the study or the subject matter of the female offender. Too much research has been encouraged, funded, and published for one to believe that there is anything like a taboo operating to curtail or regulate the questions asked and the flow of information. It is true that surprisingly little that is new can be found. The research is severely hampered by infirm or nonexistent data, and conclusions are mired in confusion and bias. Loyalists from the ranks of "the movement" seem able to find sermons even in Uniform Crime

Report figures. Those who attempt to be "objective" without demonstrating due cognizance of the subtle and not so subtle discriminatory features of the society at large (which must figure in a thorough understanding of any aspect of the society, e.g., crime or criminal justice) will miss many an important point. Still, such weaknesses, even taken together, do not a taboo make.

(2) Further, the claim that there is a relationship between feminism and female crime is irrefragable. The claim may also be trivial, but to deny any relationship is to talk nonsense.

FEMINISM AND THE FEMALE OFFENDER

However we may assess the achievements of Karl Marx—his miscalculations and excesses weighed against his startling insights and inspired (albeit naive) humanism—one cannot deny the correctness of his insistence that moral freedom (and thus moral authenticity) requires material freedom. Like every profound insight, it seems, hundreds of clear-headed critics later, an obvious and simple truth. Nevertheless, it traveled a rough route to twentieth-century understanding. When women united to form what would later be called "the feminist movement," Marx's theory about economic freedom was only a periodic thread in an elaborately woven, dark tapestry of complaints. The more pronounced threads delineated general themes of victimization and oppression, particularly victimization by men.

The "first manifesto of the liberated woman" was *The Second Sex* (de Beauvoir, 1952). It was followed a decade later by the "famous bestseller that ignited women's liberation," *The Feminine Mystique* (Friedan, 1963), then *Sexual Politics* (Millett, 1969) and *The Female Eunuch* (Greer, 1970). All of these works carried the message of female victimization by male society.

Assuming that the message of any influential document filters slowly down to mass consciousness and takes longer still to impel action, we may gauge the floruit of the movement to be roughly between the early 1960s and the 1970s. According to the Uniform Crime Reports of the Federal Bureau of Investigation, the male arrest figure for index crimes increased 55%

between 1968 and 1977. During that same period, arrests of females for index crimes increased by 201.5%. The number of women arrested for fraud during a five-year period ending in December 1978 went up 49.2%, compared to an increase for men of 13.2%. The number of women arrested for embezzlement increased 47.9%, while the number of men arrested for embezzlement rose only 1.5% (Sourcebook, 1979).

It is clear that recorded crimes by females have dramatically increased. And they are crimes of a different order than those traditionally associated with women (prostitution, shoplifting). They are crimes in the upper bracket of seriousness: violent crimes, crimes of aggression, and larceny on a large scale.

INTERPRETING THE DATA

There is no consensus regarding what these figures mean. What, if any, is the relationship between the feminist movement and female crime? When the question is asked, the answers range from the claim that the connection is a quasi-causal one to denials of any connection at all. In *Sisters in Crime,* Adler (1975a) contends that an increase in female criminality is a direct consequence of the competitive spirit and diminished inhibitions toward aggressive behavior championed by feminism. Aggressiveness is traditionally considered a masculine trait, but in the struggle for liberation it has become a trait increasingly evident in women (most feminists prefer the term "assertiveness," as it sounds less bellicose). It is primarily this malelike posture that Adler (1975b) feels explains "the rise of the female crook."

Wolfgang and many others see the rise in recorded crime as a consequence of more women having opportunities to commit crimes. Thus Winfrey (1980) quotes Wolfgang:

> As women have become more and more eligible for positions in which trust is involved, they're going to commit crimes at the same rate as men. The best index of economic progress for blacks is the rise in white-collar crime and one could say something like that for

women. Under the assumption that women have an equal proclivity to commit crimes of property, their rate of increase will be greater as they are given opportunities to do so.

Simon also focuses on increased opportunity for the types of crimes traditionally committed by women. Greater numbers of women have entered the work force, she emphasizes. Winfrey (1980) likewise quotes Simon as contending that women

> are learning skills by which they can have access to large sums of money. . . . It is not something going on in the psyche. Women now have the kinds of opportunities men have always had and are taking advantage of those opportunities.

At what might be seen as the opposite end of a continuum of responses are those who deny any connection at all between an increase in crime and the feminist movement. The very suggestion that emancipation has produced changes in female crime patterns is denounced as a plot to promote sexist stereotyping. Feinman (1979: 94) calls it a dangerous "myth . . . that misdirects and confuses investigation," and Smart (1977: 182) states that the myth is promoted primarily by "criminologists who are critical of the Women's Movement" and who are

> geared to supporting the inferior position of women in society in the naive belief that femininity is the antithesis of criminality. . . . We can see therefore that a consensus of opinion exists which serves in practice to encourage women to remain in their traditional domestic roles whilst implicitly discouraging a questioning of women's position and status.

It seems to me that a "taboolike" constraint operates to confuse and undermine serious inquiry. The liberated view—espoused by all who strive not to be labeled "mean spirited or reactionary bigots" (see May, 1980)—contends that the natural gender condition is androgynous. Those sex differences which may be identified are either trivial or superficial in that they are wholly the result of social conditioning. Adelson (1980), in a review of May's book, writes:

> Because there is very little evidence to support any of these beliefs, the case is often made not by argument but by intimidation.... Though a great many topics in psychology are now politicized, nowhere is the ideological bias more entrenched, more unabashed and more arrogant than in the study of gender.
>
> To question these ideas is to risk jeers and hissing when the issues are discussed in public and a torrent of abusive letters when they are debated in print. When a psychological topic becomes so completely hostage to ideology, we lose any capacity to think about it freshly or in depth. *Contention absorbs all our intellectual energy* [emphasis added].

Nowhere has the contention been more evident than in discussions of female criminality. The opponents of the women's liberation movement are always eager to seize upon examples of the trouble that equal rights might bring, ranging from an increase of cancer among women to the threat of military service (with the possibility of unisex restrooms falling somewhere in the middle). The claim that emancipation has brought about an increase in female crime goes to the core of feminist doctrine and ignites a flame over the very dry timber of yesterday's battlefield.

Whatever merit a thesis of causality may lack is compensated for by the drama of the challenge presented to the polemic camps. Feminists did not miss the cue. It was a call to arms—a call to defend the liberated front against the encroachment of ancient tyrannies. The appearance of an enemy has an energizing effect on any movement. This movement, having won some battles, was winding down. Where once had been the inspiration of a fine-sounding reveille, the movement lately resonated with dissonant grousing—as though, startled at having won the point of a major argument, leaders had lost their train of thought. The suggestion that an increase in female crime is a consequence of the movement restored attention.

Both positions in this lively exchange rely on the Uniform Crime Reports for strength. However, as with most statistics, these can be used to support either side. The UCR represents data collected by the Federal Bureau of Investigation on arrests nationwide. A great deal of interpretation is necessary to translate the collected figures into an appraisal of the crime situation.

LIBERATION AND OPPORTUNITIES

An understanding of the relationship between female crime and the feminist movement is not to be found in facts and figures. In the juxtaposition of "women's liberation" and increased rates of reported crime, it is important to note that liberation is not a sufficient cause. The opportunities for crime which are part of an overall increase in opportunity fought for and won by the feminist movement supply only the *necessary* conditions for crime. But to answer the larger critical question of why some people respond to an opportunity by exploiting it for criminal possibilities and others do not is to probe the *sufficient* determinants of criminal behavior, male or female.

Consistent with that distinction, we might suppose that the feminist movement has contributed to female criminality in two ways: (1) by expanding a woman's career opportunities, giving her a lease on a Madison Avenue boutique or keys to the executive board room, and multiplying the possibilities for illegality; and (2) through encouraging the breakdown of inhibitions toward aggressive behavior.

How far does that take us, given that feminism is primarily a middle- and upper-class movement, while offenders are primarily from the underprivileged classes? Furthermore, research, however sparse, indicates that female offenders do not necessarily share the sentiments of the movement (Giordano and Cernkovich, 1979). Feminism has not increased the economic opportunities of women who are without skills or resources. The obvious effect of feminism on crime occurs toward the other end of the scale. It is known that increasing numbers of women have had opportunities to commit "white-collar crimes" and that such crime has increased among women. Compared with the 1.5% increase in embezzlement arrests among men, the figure for women shows a 47.9% increase. Fraud arrests increased 49.2% in a five-year period among women, compared to 13.2% among men. No daring theoretical leap is required to assert that these facts are connected. Whether the women who commit such crimes are themselves feminists is irrelevant. Feminism has given them opportunities they would not otherwise have had.

We cannot, however, rule out the possibility that feminism has also contributed to the growth in crime among lower-class women. It has not done so by broadening their economic horizons, and it did not necessarily give them a rationale *which they accept* for emulating the aggressiveness of men. But it may well have affected them without their accepting the ideology or even being aware of it as a movement. It may have done this merely by providing them with examples of successful, free, gutsy, independent women.

The other way that the movement and these UCR figures are related may be simply that law enforcement officers are more willing, when faced with a less helpless image of womanhood, to arrest women. In terms of white-collar crimes, especially, the figures alone tell us very little, since white-collar crime has been a loosely prosecuted category until fairly recently. So it may be that such crimes are on the rise because they have become more serious in the eyes of law enforcement. Clearly, if companies that overlooked white-collar crime in the past, no longer overlook it, more complaints will ensue, more charges will be made, and more arrests will be recorded in UCR. But that may or may not reflect an actual rise in white-collar crime. It may reflect only a lowering of the tolerance level for those crimes.

The same thing may be happening across the board in terms of arrests of female offenders. Women have always been held to be responsible for guarding chastity, sexual virtue, and the institution of the nuclear family. Those women who conduct themselves in a way that appears to demonstrate that they have abandoned that guardianship have always been severely chastised by the law (Singer, 1973; Gallagher, 1979; Smart, 1977). Perhaps, as women are now seen by male society as having responsibility for some of the economic and financial institutions outside the conjugal relationship, law enforcement no longer hesitates to act in cases where that (newly acquired) responsibility is abused.

RETURNING TO TABOO

To bring us back to the subject of taboo, one might reasonably ask why anyone would think that there is not a relationship between this dramatic change in opportunities, role expectations, behavior, and attitudes and what is theatrically referred to as "the dark side of personal behavior." Is there an assumption that women are made of rarefied material, immune to the temptations to which men succumb? If that is the assumption, it is indeed an odd one, given the aforementioned relentless insistence by feminists that we must rid ourselves of the tendency to assume that certain clusters of traits (or virtues) belong to women and others to men. Essential to the emancipation struggle has been the removal of those limits which constrain individual choices, and specifically those limits which constrain by the force of restrictive definitions of the female sex role. And yet, indeed, we were told by its leaders that the feminist movement would lead to a decrease in crime and generally to a less violent society (DeCrow, 1976). The forecast was predicated on the conviction that women have been the target of male oppression and that liberation would automatically bring an improved world.

The construction of male villainy was crucial to the mobilization of feminism. Like waving a red flag, it provided a focal point on which to project accumulated resentment and "astral discontent." The historical interest in the female criminal has consistently reinforced either the myth of the evil woman whose inherent skill at deception and manipulation explained her role in criminal activity, or the idea that women were unstable and constitutionally prone to impulse, not unlike children. Common to all the prevailing literature is the assumption that women are fundamentally and qualitatively different from men. Though unique in every way, they have been studied only in relationship to men, that is, as sexual mates, wives, and mothers. What the feminist movement has done is conform to the paradigm, except that the woman now is invariably a crushed instead of a fallen woman. The important thing, however, remains—woman as related to man.

No terms could better describe the stereotype of the good/bad woman trapped in artificial morality patterns than those employed in Freud's assertion that a taboo is characterized by awe and aversion. It took a great deal of consciousness raising for women to grasp the full extent of the crippling consequences of that stereotype. But women are not much ahead if they only exchange one stereotype for another—that of the good or bad woman for that of victim.

There seems to be a creeping authoritarianism which on the one hand allows for blatant contradictions and on the other resists any evidence of the irreducible ambiguities in human—therefore in female—behavior. Women have traditionally been sheltered, protected, and cared for in ways that curtailed and often tragically precluded the fulfillment of their potential. To the extent that this was a conspiracy, women were certainly co-conspirators.

Women accepted the protection of men under laws that limited options. They accepted protection not only from rape (see Brownmiller, 1975) but from freedom—from the terrors of existential freedom. When women realized that the price was too high, that it would be paid in self-loathing, bitterness, and waste of potential, they began to wrest from men control of their lives, to struggle to become independent and autonomous.

The outraged claim of victimization and betrayal was a powerful rallying cry, and it served women well. They were able to consolidate forces, articulate grievances, and state important minimal requirements necessary to put women on an equal footing with men (as a class).[2] That seems to be an extraordinary tale of historical progress—late and slow, but genuine progress.

What is not good is that this creeping bad faith exerts pressure to have things all ways. Armies of strident women now march toward the Wall Street of their fantasies keeping step with the how-dare-you-look-at-me-as-a-sex-symbol-when-what-I-want-now-is-to-be-president-of-the-corporation beat of entitlement.[3] We cannot say both that nothing but cultural expectation bars us from taking on traditionally male-held positions and that in the course of exposure to the frustrations, temptations, competition, and strain of the labor market we will somehow remain pure where (lesser?) males succumb. If in removing the normative constraints upon women it was necessary to shout from the rooftops that a spade is a spade, it is not proper to qualify that now with "until and unless we say it is a hoe."

Women cannot, or anyhow should not, claim that there is nothing constitutionally different about them which is relevant to their assimilation into the labor market—insisting that they can perform with equal competence and vigor whatever tasks men performed, yet that they will be (somehow constitutionally) impervious to the frustrations, pressures, and temptations which corrupt men.

WOMEN AS OFFENDERS AND VICTIMS

So the image of the female offender, especially one who is clearly a victimizer, is difficult to square with the important image of woman as victim. But then, the complexity of human behavior is always difficult to square with rigid stereotypes. That is what today's problem comes to.

Of course, not everyone would so narrowly argue the case for victimized women. Nevertheless, the victim image continues to have talismanic importance in feminist literature. One reason for the influence and pervasiveness of the victim image stems from its enormous success and clout in the legitimate context of rape.

Until the 1960s, the crime of rape was largely borne by the victim in silence. It was indeed a taboo topic. Women were helpless and ashamed, the law was wholly inadequate, and the dimensions of the crime were only beginning to be contemplated. The considerable progress, in terms of sensitizing the public and law enforcement personnel, correcting some of the brutally prejudicial antiquated laws, expansion of services to the rape victim, requiring previously withheld cooperation from hospitals and the medical profession, all began with a tremendously successful campaign by feminists.[4]

However, like so many emotionally potent terms, "rape" was so charged with energy that it was exploited and made to do work that had little connection with its lexical meaning. It soon not only referred to the heinous crime itself, but was called upon to describe the most banal interactions between men and women. "Little rapes" came to mean any discomfort a woman might feel in the presence of lustful men who failed totally to disguise all sexual interest. No overt move, but only the most subtle suggestion of sexuality was necessary to constitute an affront to this newly awakened, delicate sensibility. These "little rapes" not only made everyone nervous (the anxious burden of proof was on all men, and it was relentless), but the easy distortion of the lexical usage deprived the term of its seriousness and true horror.

Any number of other words could serve to illustrate this tendency to stretch a perfectly workable term beyond its intended usage. Prostitution, for example, has for some time carried the burden of describing any exchange of service in which the servicer feels a degree less than total fulfillment of his or her full creative potential, and we all know what fate "the politics of . . ." has suffered. The term "victim" is just such a word. It has a perfectly clear, ordinary-language usage, and its referent is a person who suffers a destructive, injurious action; usually the victim is cheated by the dishonesty of others. To the extent that women have been duped or swindled on the social scale, as we have been expected to believe, and permitting the kind of generalization feminists insist upon, they have been willing dupes.

The fact is that women have not been and are not now victims of male oppression. Middle- and upper-class women have had numerous privileges, extraordinary leisure, and have been remarkably pampered and protected (as a class) by men, and the feminist movement is primarily a middle- and upper-class movement of just such privileged, leisured, pampered, and protected women.[5]

Women made compromises and participated in tradeoffs to obtain a handle on power, prestige, and material goods. For some the bargain was more fortunate and felicitous than for others. If women were betrayed and victimized, then so were men. But if the word "victim" is stretched to cover all cases of human misery, then, of course, it loses its usefulness.

Moreover, narrow explanations lead to limited understanding. One wonders whether there remain serious half truths which stand as obstacles to the goal of equality for women. To assume the burden of guilt or responsibility for whatever oppressive conditions women have endured is not to diminish the tragedy of narrow lives. It is to reapportion the blame (if blame is even relevant). To assume that women are responsible agents is to afford them the dignity which is a precondition to the autonomy and responsible independence they seek.

An abandonment of the image of betrayed innocent, victim, and martyr opens the way for a less defensive examination and analysis of the manifold varieties of female behavior. Within such infinite varieties, there will inevitably be responses to the opportunity for crime that will parallel men's responses to such opportunities.

That is, after all, at least part of what is meant by equality.

NOTES

1. A sexual fetish is a good example of this mechanism, as it results from the inability to cope with the whole person; hence, some part or aspect of the person or a thing representing it becomes the focal point and source of excitement.

2. The major goals of the movement can be reduced to four: (1) equal treatment under the law; (2) protection from discrimination on the basis of sex; (3) physical self-determination; and (4) political and economic power for women as a class (from Eastwood, 1979).

3. The phrase "sense of entitlement" was coined by Coleman (1961), who uses it to refer to the assumption of privilege that he found to be common among the indulged, highly privileged adolescents.

4. This is not meant to suggest that the problem of rape is in the past, but only that progress has been made.

5. It ought to go without saying, but will not, that poor women, on the other hand, *are* victims of society's injustices. But so are poor men.

REFERENCES

ADELSON, J. (1980) Review of "Sex and Fantasy," by R. May. New York Times Book Review (March 9): p. 3ff.

ADLER, F. (1975a) Sisters in Crime: The Rise of the New Female Criminal. New York: McGraw-Hill.

——— (1975b) "The rise of the female crook." Psychology Today 9 (November): p. 42ff.

BECKER, E. (1964) Revolution in Psychiatry. New York: Macmillan.

——— (1973) The Denial of Death. New York: Macmillan.

BROWNMILLER, S. (1975) Against Our Will. New York: Simon and Schuster.

COLEMAN, J. S. (1961) The Adolescent Society. New York: Macmillan.

DE BEAUVOIR, S. (1952) The Second Sex. New York: Knopf.

DeCROW, K. (1976) Presented at the Conference on Women and Crime, February 26-27.

EASTWOOD, M. (1979) "Feminism and the law," in J. Freeman (ed.) Women: A Feminist Perspective. Palo Alto, CA: Mayfield.

FEINMAN, C. (1979) "Sex role stereotypes and justice for women." Crime and Delinquency 25: 87-94.

FREUD, S. (1946) Totem and Taboo. New York: Vintage.

FRIEDAN, B. (1963) The Feminine Mystique. New York: Dell.

GALLAGHER, M. J. (1979) "Fascinating contradictions: the law's myths about women." New Jersey Lawyer 88 (August): 12-15.

GIORDANO, P. C., and S. A. CERNKOVICH (1979) "On complicating the relationship between liberation and delinquency." Social Problems 26: 467-481.

GREER, G. (1970) The Female Eunuch. New York: McGraw-Hill.

MAY, R. (1980) Sex and Fantasy: Patterns of Male and Female Development. New York: Norton.

MILLETT, K. (1969) Sexual Politics. New York: Doubleday.

SINGER, L. (1973) "Women and the correctional process." Amer. Criminal Law Rev. 11 (Winter): 295-308.

SMART, C. (1977) Women, Crime and Criminology: A Feminist Critique. London: Routledge and Kegan Paul.

Sourcebook of Criminal Justice Statistics (1979) Criminal Justice Research Center, Albany, NY.

WINFREY, C. (1980) "White-collar crimes by women: why are they on the rise?" New York Times (January 21): A18.

5

Andrew Karmen

John Jay College of Criminal Justice

RACE, INFERIORITY, CRIME, AND RESEARCH TABOOS

> Are blacks more prone to crime than whites, Jews or Irishmen than Germans or Englishmen, immigrants than the native born? There is a persistent tendency to regard with suspicion those of different origins, to try to assert their inferiority in intelligence, morality or both. To enter into open discussion of links between race and crime is to enter a minefield. Politically, the issue is dynamite. Claims that certain ethnic groups are inferior have served, throughout history, to justify all kinds of persecution, oppression, exploitation. So powerful is the reaction now, from the oppressed and their champions, that it is hard to investigate or discuss such issues without arousing strong feelings.
>
> Radzinowicz and King (1977: 23)

Criminologists now confront a controversy that has spilled over from sociology, psychology, biology, and education. The subject is the supposed interrelationships among race, IQ, and crime. The issue is whether or not there are taboos that inhibit research. Each side in the debate denounces its opponents for being unscientific and for selectively choosing evidence to support their political ideology. Those who believe that research into racial differences in intelligence is tabooed charge that blacks are less intelligent than whites but that whites in high places conspire to cover up this finding. Those who think that research into the link between intelligence and criminality is forbidden contend that lawbreakers are not as smart as law-abiders and that criminologists in positions of responsibility suppress this finding too.

The argument has been presented in its crudest, most unabashed form by Weyl (1973). Writing in an international journal devoted to studies of race and heredity in which his article was sandwiched between articles on racial differences in brain sizes, Weyl claimed that he had solved the "riddle of excessive black criminality." Environmental explanations that centered on the indignities of oppression and the injustices of discrimination were refuted by the facts. Weyl (1973: 46-48) observed, "The most obvious characteristic which Negroes and criminals have in common is below average intelligence." Citing research findings from years of mental testing, he stated that "one could conclude that the average white convict was dull, but not feeble-minded, whereas the average black inmate was a moron."

Weyl complained that the relationship between criminality and low intelligence had been known for decades, but the evidence expunged from modern criminology texts. Furthermore, he claimed, the implications of this connection for repressing crime had been ignored:

> One of the causes of the frightening and continuous rise in the American crime rate may be the tendency to seek to dissuade potential criminals from antisocial conduct by reason, persuasion and appeasement in cases where their intelligence levels are so low that the threat of retribution is the only efficacious deterrent.

A first reaction to Weyl's charges might be that they have some basis, the subject is tabooed, but the self-evident relationships he cites have been deemphasized for justifiable reasons: to protect the innocent, to help the disadvantaged, to avoid stigmatization. But a closer inspection of the accusations will show that they have no foundation. He establishes no simple, straightforward associations between race and intelligence, between intelligence and crime, or between race and crime. Each of these three variables can be defined and measured in a manipulative way to produce the desired outcome. Most important, the political implications of Weyl's arguments are without merit: minorities are not receiving preferential treatment (the alleged reality of their inferiority is not suppressed), and criminals are not coddled (punishment has always been a central feature of the criminal justice system).

Devastating critiques have been leveled against attempts to malign various racial or ethnic groups as intellectually inferior. The unsound logic behind the construction, administration, and interpretation of the IQ test and its equation with intelligence has been thoroughly examined (see the collections edited by Montagu, 1975; Senna, 1973; and Block and Dworkin, 1976). The race, delinquency, and IQ association has been well explored (Empey, 1978: 208-217; Vold, 1979: 89-97).

Concerning the alleged link between race and crime, Richard Korn and Lloyd McCorkle (1959: 231-232) reminded those who sought to explore this connection that the social definition of race could not be used in biologically oriented studies. Race would have to be treated as a quantitative rather than a qualitative variable. Crime statistics drawn from the inadequate, oversimplified, popular notion of just two alternatives, black or white, would have to be adjusted for persons of mixed parentage. The net effect of this genetically more accurate procedure would be to transfer a considerable number of crimes and criminals from the category labeled "black" to middle-ground categories, or to reassign some percentage of the crimes and criminals who were partly white to the "white" column. Methodologically and practically, these corrections would become impossible to implement, because racial heritage is in actuality a spectrum or continuum, and most people are not able to calculate their true position on it. The net effect is that racial comparisons based on hereditarian principles are precluded.

The validity of race-specific crime statistics was seriously questioned by Sagarin (1967: 11), who asked, "Is white crime crime?" Official statistics never counted—and still do not keep track of—the mass participation by whites in crimes against blacks, from the lynchings of the past to the coverups of illegal discriminatory acts today. If the astronomically high actual white crime rate were calculated, then the liberal environmentalist prediction that under comparable conditions blacks have essentially the same crime rate as whites would become a profoundly pessimistic forecast.

Throughout the development of criminology, many heated debates have erupted over misleading data, erroneous interpretations, and illogical conclusions. But the race and inferiority debate, and the emerging controversies over inferiority and crime and racial inferiority and crime become particularly bitter because of the profound social-policy implications that surround the acceptance or rejection of competing, mutually contradictory explanations of the same data. The historical record provides ample warnings about the serious repercussions of popular misunderstandings of the causes of and cures for crime. Theories about lawbreakers as defective beings and notions about entire races being inherently inferior and particularly crime-prone have been present in criminology since its inception. The convergence between these threads of criminological thought and political doctrines has been exploited by social movements seeking to implement repressive measures with dire consequences for many individuals and for entire groups.

Since those who forget the lessons of the past are doomed to repeat the mistakes of previous generations, it is imperative to (briefly) review: (1) some early ideas about race and inferiority in criminology; (2) crime control policies that flowed from these theories; and (3) the history of the charge that research taboos impede inquiries into racial differences in intelligence levels and crime rates.

THE RISE OF SCIENTIFIC RACISM AND ELITISM

The origins of scientific racism and elitism can be traced back to the earliest applications of Darwin's theory of evolution to human society. Social Darwinists speculated about which individuals and groups were throwbacks to more primitive types. These early social scientists sought to identify atavisms and reversions—long-lost characteristics that would provide criteria for rating and ranking people. Darwin's own remark that there was a "rather wide gap . . . between say a Hottentot and an Orang" set off waves of conjecture about missing links between primitive African tribes and apes. Although most European scientists considered the superiority of Caucasians self-evident, even the most naive researchers tried to demonstrate this empirically. For example, Herbert Spencer, the leading proponent of "survival of the fittest" policies, believed that "civilized" men had larger skulls and more developed nervous systems than "savages" (Rennie, 1978: 64-65).

The Italian Positivist School wove together two lines of inquiry; the search for a criminal type and the quest for proof of racial superiority and inferiority. The synthesis was succinctly expressed by Cesare Lombroso:

> The principal thing is always ... the stifling of the primitive wild instincts. Even if he (the Negro) is dressed in the European way and has accepted the customs of modern culture, all too often there remains in him the lack of respect for the life of his fellow men, the disregard for life which all wild people have in common. To them, a murder appears as an ordinary occurrence, even a glorious occurrence when it is inspired by feelings of vengeance. This mentality is furthered in the Negro by his scorn of his fellow white citizens, and by bestial sexual impulses. [Quoted by Bonger, 1943: 48-49].

The biological determinism of the positivists proposed that physique, character, and behavior were intimately related, although subject to social influences. Their assertions that criminals were born, not made, and were primitive evolutionary types stranded on the lower rungs of the ladder of perfection brought them into sharp conflict with strict environmentalists. At the Second International Congress on Criminal Anthropology in Paris in 1889, the confrontations were so heated that leading biological determinists did not attend the third one (Quinney, 1979: 56).

The idea that "imbeciles" and "idiots" would be unable to resist criminal impulses—or even distinguish right from wrong—was a revision of the positivists' "born criminal" thesis from physical types to mental types (Hirschi and Hindelang, 1977: 583).

Prison doctor Charles Goring examined 3000 male convicts in England in order to establish a new criminology based upon scientifically verifiable facts. He concluded that Lombroso was mistaken about the existence of a born physical criminal type. But convicts could be distinguished from noncriminals by their defective physique as indicated by stature and body weight, and by their defective mental capacity as measured by general intelligence tests. Goring contended that defective intelligence due to poor heredity was the cause of delinquent behavior and that environmental forces were of little importance compared to inheritance (Quinney and Wildeman, 1977: 60-61; Empey, 1978: 209).

Psychologist Henry Goddard studied "criminal imbeciles" in training schools. He found that at least 25% —perhaps as many as 75%—of all delinquents were mentally defective. Even though not all the feebleminded were criminals, the high proportion of imbeciles among criminals led him to propose that to control crime the mentally defective should be prevented from propagating. He estimated that two-thirds of mental defectives inherited their condition from degenerate parents (Rennie, 1978: 83; Empey, 1978: 210).

A study of "criminal intelligence" was conducted by Murchison (1926), who administered mental tests to both prisoners and guards. He discovered that the prisoners scored substantially higher on these tests. He then broke down the prisoners' results by nativity, race, and sex, and found differences but dismissed them as unimportant. He condemned a "maternalistic" attitude toward criminals that coddled the young, feebleminded, and insane, and he urged sure, swift, and severe punishment as the antidote to crime waves. He recommended the abolition of juries, bail, probation, and parole and the application of mandatory capital punishment to habitual criminals, regardless of age or mental ability.

Schlapp and Smith (1928) sought to nurture the development of a new criminology based on medical and biological principles. They associated nervous and glandular disorders in mothers with feeblemindedness in their children, and mental defectiveness with certain types of delinquent and criminal behaviors. They warned that feeblemindedness had to be recognized, treated, and prevented if Western civilization were to survive. They condemned the "paternalistic" system that kept alive countless millions of "defectives and weaklings" who would have perished in infancy or childhood under "natural" conditions, and they advocated the rejection of a 'false humanitarianism" that preserved vast armies of the "worthless and dependent," who dragged down the mean of the nation's culture and its "racial capacity." Genetic principles should guide human affairs, they urged, and the unfit should be sterilized, despite the "roar" that will arise from leaders of creeds and races of "inferior stocks and strata."

Similarly, Terman, a pioneer of mental testing, emphasized that feebleminded persons were potential criminals. Educational psychologist Thorndike explicitly associated greater intelligence with higher morality and lesser intelligence with viciousness, and urged that the "able and good" beget and rear children while the vicious and inferior be sterilized. Because the liberal tradition from Jefferson onward assumed a tie between talent and virtue, it simply followed that those with less talent would have less virtue (Karier, 1972).

THE POLITICIZATION OF
SCIENTIFIC RACISM AND ELITISM

The development of criminological thought about race and crime, race and inferiority, inferiority and crime, and racial inferiority and crime did not occur in a social vacuum. Crime theories were strongly influenced by and had an impact on the dominant political currents of their time.

The biological determinism of the Italian Positivist School was able to permeate the mainstream of early criminological theory for a number of reasons unrelated to strict scientific merit; its image as a new empirical approach borrowed the prestige of natural science. Respected figures such as physicians, psychologists, lawyers, and magistrates embraced and expounded a set of similar beliefs, its fundamental premises were rooted in tradition and superstition, its teaching about innate superiority and inferiority resonated with national chauvinist claims, and its crime prevention programs legitimated the extension of state power (Quinney, 1979: 56).

The application of Darwin's evolutionary principles to human society was used to justify the growing gap between the often predatory rich and the toiling poor, as well as the exploitation and oppression of colonial peoples by industrializing capitalist nations. Thé concepts of greater and lesser races and of fit and unfit individuals found their way into criminological thought as politically useful explanations of lawabiding versus lawbreaking behavior.

In the late 1800s, the "child savers," responsible for developing the juvenile justice system, equated the "dangerous classes" with the "criminal classes" and looked upon them with a mixture of contempt and benevolence. Crime was pictured as rising from the "lowest orders" and engulfing "respectable society" like a virulent plague. Dugdale's series of papers on crime, pauperism, and disease in the Jukes family was distorted almost beyond recognition by anti-intellectual supporters of hereditarian theories of crime. The image of criminals as less than human creatures living in burrows, dens, and slime was strongly influenced and aggravated by nativist and racist doctrines. Some child savers advocated drastic measures such as cutting off and drying up the supply of unfortunates destined to lead lives of lawlessness by registering them and then sterilizing or permanently incarcerating them. But overly fatalistic genetic programs were largely rejected in favor of cautiously optimistic plans to neutralize dangerous inborn tendencies by reaching and rescuing little waifs at the first signs of trouble (Platt, 1974).

The most significant convergence between criminological thought about race, intelligence, and crime and a political movement came about during the early decades of this century. Eugenics incorporated themes from the mental testing movement, the progressive movement, social Darwinism, the child savers, and biocriminology and synthesized them into a plausible pseudoscientific program that had wide popular appeal, prestigious backers, and barbaric consequences.

The professed aim of eugenicists was human betterment and racial improvement through the application of biological knowledge to social problems. Positive eugenics involved encouraging people from higher classes with superior intelligence and loftier morality to multiply fruitfully. Negative eugenics meant discouraging or preventing unworthy parenthood in order to eliminate undesirable traits from the gene pool. A leading eugenicist estimated that 10% of the American population were social misfits who carried bad genes for insanity, criminality, delinquency, feeblemindedness, alcoholism, pauperism, dependency, and various physical ailments. Since illegal, immoral, and degenerate behaviors from prostitution to murder were suspected of being genetically determined, sterilization was considered the solution. Bills were introduced which called for the sterilization of prostitutes, auto thieves, and people who stole chickens (Karier, 1972: 159).

At the movement's peak in the aftermath of the First World War, eugenics courses were taught at three-quarters of the nation's colleges and universities. A number of institutes conducted eugenics research, and many scholarly journals and popular magazines publicized their findings. Sterilization laws and antimiscegenation statutes prohibiting interracial marriages in accordance with eugenics principles were passed in thirty states. Concerns about inherently crime-prone races and ethnic groups and fears about feebleminded foreigners who failed IQ tests (given in English) were bandied about by congressmen before they enacted the Immigration Restriction Act of 1924 (Allen, 1974: 35).

Eugenics zealots scorned the "idiotic public," equated lower class status with inferior genes, and exalted their own upper-middle class and upper-class ancestry as the fount of virtually all human progress. Vulgarizing Darwin, they postulated a simple ranking of races from the lowest, Negro, to the highest, Caucasian. Of white ethnic groups, the Nordics were deemed superior mentally and physically. Southern and Eastern European nationalities were thought to be saddled with undesirable traits, resistant to assimilation, unappreciative of American ideals, and prone to have large families (Ludmerer, 1972: 20-27).

Until the mid 1920s, no geneticists of any reputation—and only one distinguished anthropologist—publicly disputed these racist and elitist preachings cloaked in scientific terminology. An important nucleus of experimental geneticists brought the eugenics movement an aura of credibility and respectability. Case studies of notorious clans plagued from one generation to another along every branch of their family trees by "degeneracy" were cited as evidence of the imminent dangers of unchecked procreation by the unfit. Eugenics propagandists portrayed themselves as radical reformers on a crusade to save the world from "menaces to civilization" and "race suicide." Their promises of a "utopia of supermen" were echoed by politicians and business leaders who clamored for the immediate translation of biological findings into legislative decrees before the forces of anarchy took command (Ludmerer, 1972: 28-36).

Hitler was a strong advocate of eugenics policies, and upon his advent to power the German eugenics movement became inextricably identified with the Nazi regime. In 1933, German hereditary health courts with state-appointed doctors and judges began to implement the Eugenic Sterilization Law on a massive scale. Some leading American eugenicists praised these efforts to ensure that inferior members of the Third Reich would not burden its future. But many American geneticists had great reservations. Cautious and skeptical, these scientists felt uncomfortable in a movement that so exaggerated the role of heredity and so belittled the importance of environment. A few at a time, they began to disassociate and disaffiliate themselves from and to repudiate their previous stands. Most spoke out individually. Some worked to change the editorial policies of journals and magazines. Others tried to pass a resolution condemning racism at an international congress of geneticists (the Genetics Society of America never formally denounced eugenics policies or Nazi racism). These professionals, anxious to restore the aura of objectivity to their discipline, began to promulgate for the first time a doctrine of the social responsibility of the scientist: to inform the public of research findings whenever science and technology were applied to social issues; to recognize the limitations of science and research; to distinguish between their knowledge as scientists and their personal opinions as citizens; and to avoid public advocacy and policy making. What the geneticists were doing, albeit implicitly, was reasserting the internal autonomy of their discipline. They could no longer pretend to be immune to social pressures, but they could try to maintain their own stndards of proof and truth (Ludmerer, 1972: 115-129).

SCIENTIFIC RACISM AND
ELITISM ON THE DEFENSIVE

During the 1930s, a dramatic transformation took place. Crude, overt racism and elitism were no longer fashionable in enlightened circles.

In the face of fascist aggression, American scientists began to speak out through their professional organizations. Anthropologists condemned the jingoism and narrowmindedness of the eugenics movement. Psychologists refuted the ranking of races by intelligence that some eugenicists popularized.

Sutherland was the first prominent American criminologist to challenge the orthodoxy of the discipline that linked low intelligence with crime. He debunked "mental testers" and established the fundamental critique followed by most criminologists since his early essay on the subject (Sutherland, 1931). He contended that intelligence tests measure "test intelligence," which is culturally defined, and that criminal behavior, like lawabiding behavior, is socially learned rather than innately determined.

Tulchin (1939) carried out a sophisticated multivariate analysis of possible relationships among a host of factors, including intelligence and criminality. He tested prisoners in Illinois and compared their scores to local Army draftees. The proportion of prisoners with below normal or inferior scoring was very similar to that of soldiers—roughly 25%. There were substantial differences among prisoners by nativity, race, and type of crime. Although men of all grades of intelligence were found in each of his seven crime categories, those who were imprisoned for fraud had the highest test scores, while those incarcerated for sex crimes had the lowest average score. Intelligence seemed to play an important role in influencing the type of crime committed rather than in determining criminality itself.

Bonger (1943) reported that by the eve of the Second World War, mainstream American criminologists had accepted the thesis that environmental conditions—not inherent traits—accounted for the high rate of black street crime. Ironically, Bonger himself did not reject the premise that led to the conclusion he opposed. He wrote that he had the impression, but was not certain, that besides very different environmental influences, IQ test results indicated that blacks were by birth less intelligent than whites. But, he argued, everyday experience confirmed that great intelligence was no guarantee of good character. A basic truth in criminology was that smartness primarily restrained people from committing "dumb" crimes.

In the late 1930s, research into human genetics nearly came to a standstill in the United States. In addition to numerous technical impediments, the close association of the discipline with the waning eugenics movement and the growing fascist threat inhibited research by biologists who feared their findings would be carelessly—or cleverly—twisted to fit totalitarian ends (Ludmerer, 1972: 35-36).

The Harvard anthropologist Hooton continued to search for born criminals. Although Hooton linked physical abnormalities to mental inferiority and these defects to lawlessness, he did not connect crime and inferiority with race. In fact, he condemned "the malignant nonsense" about racial psychology that emanated from those who tried to justify the oppression of ethnic minorities (Hooton, 1939: 129). At the same time, he called for the extirpation of the mentally, morally, and physically unfit.

Rennie (1978: 92) pronounced the eugenics movement dead, buried in the mass graves of Auschwitz, Buchenwald, and Dachau along with the unnumbered millions Hitler targeted for elimination: the Jews, the gypsies, and all those deemed by the Nazis to be inferior human stock. The Third Reich, with its selective breeding and its zeal to exterminate "mongrel" races, was the ultimate eugenic experiment, and it dealt a fatal blow to the respectability of the movement. In the social sciences particularly it became unacceptable to ask whether one race was superior to another—either in terms of intelligence quotients or crime rates. The prevailing orthodoxy had changed.

SCIENTIFIC RACISM AND ELITISM REVIVES

The smoldering issues of race and inferiority and of inferiority and crime have been rekindled by distinguished scientists at prestigious universities. They began to challenge what they perceived as research taboos and insisted that issues which many scientists considered resolved be returned to the agenda. They portrayed themselves as underdogs, voices in the wilderness, champions of the truth, and victims of an establishment conspiracy of silence.

The physiologist Sheldon, of the University of Chicago and Columbia, introduced European somatotype theories to the United States in 1949. He practiced constitutional psychology and psychiatry based on a study of body structure in order to predict temperament and character. Sheldon developed a scale that made it possible to classify individuals with the same precision as a judge awarding points at an animal show. Based on experiences at livestock exhibits as well as his scientific training, he devised a "t component" which he called "thoroughbredness." Delinquent youths were categorized as "of extraordinarily poor stock and low t." Sheldon observed that at the heart of all theories of constitutional psychology was an issue that most social scientists failed to acknowledge—the varying physical quality of human material (Rennie, 1978: 221-222). He contended that, since delinquency is mainly in the germ plasm, the only hope for controlling it lies in selective breeding to weed out harmful constitutional types (Sheldon, 1949: 872).

A former member of the staff of the United States Military Academy at West Point, McGurk (1956: 92) summarized his views about racial psychology:

> If we in America are going to make any sense out of the Supreme Court's desegregation decision, we will have to be more factual about race differences and much less emotional.

> As far as psychological differences between Negroes and whites are concerned, we have wished—and dreamed—that there were no such differences. We have identified this wish with reality, and on it have established a race relations policy that was so clearly a failure that we had to appeal to distorting propaganda for its support. When that, too, failed, we appealed to the legal machinery to do what nature was not content to do.

> These differences are not the result of differences in social and economic opportunities, and they will not disappear as the social and economic opportunities of Negroes and whites are equalized.

McGurk concluded that additional research was needed, but that it was becoming more and more likely that, instead, speculation and distortion would predominate in the years ahead.

The efforts of Putnam (1961: 49-50) to address the issues of race and reason quickly turned into a tirade against the civil-rights movement. He evoked a specter of deliberate behind-the-scenes equalitarian coverups of the reality of superior and inferior races:

> In a moral sense we are confronted with what might almost be called a trilogy of conspiracy, fraud and intimidation: conspiracy to gain control of important citadels of learning and news dissemination, fraud in the teaching of false racial doctrines, and intimidation in suppressing those who would preach the truth.

At about the same time, Ingle (1961: 73), chairman of the psychology department of the University of Chicago and editor of a science journal, asked, "Is science to continue as the free pursuit of knowledge, or is it to become subordinate to social and political theories?" He urged that there be no rules to stop debate and inquiry about genetic differences between races. An "egalitarian dogma" had developed, he contended, which was a prime example of "scientism—the simplistic and reductive treatment of a complex scientific question." Egalitarians who had a strong emotional investment in their beliefs were quick to brand anyone who expressed doubts or sought additional information as "racists."

The former chairman of the department of psychology at Columbia University and past president of the American Psychological Association, Garrett (1961) observed that many once believed "the Negro race to be less natively gifted than the white . . . to be less intelligent and more indolent . . . and to be somewhat lacking in the fundamental traits of honesty and reliability." But social scientists today rejected these "one-time common sense judgments" in favor of beliefs that racial differences are only skin deep, that all races are potentially equal in ability but differ in motivations and opportunities to achieve due to prejudice and discrimination. He claimed an "equalitarian dogma" had caught on among "humanitarians, social reformers, crusaders, sentimentalists, and even some politicians." Americans were being subjected to a barrage of propaganda unrivaled in its intensity and its self-righteousness. The doctrine was being spread by the media, anthropologists under the influence of Boas, theologians, civil-rights groups inspired by the 1954 school desegregation decision, and "last, but by no means least, the Communists . . . who use racial conflicts to foment trouble." Garrett contended that "Hitler's unspeakable cruelties and the absurd racial superiority theories of the Nazis" fostered a favorable climate for equalitarianism to take root, and he concluded (1961: 72-73):

> Surely there are no scientific reasons why restrictions should be placed on further research. The equalitarian dogma at best represents a sincere if misguided effort to help the Negro by ignoring or even suppressing evidence of his mental and social immaturity. At worst the equalitarian dogma is the scientific hoax of the century.

In 1966, Garrett asserted, "I welcome every honest effort to help Negroes improve their lot but I do not believe it is necessary to 'prove' that no racial differences exist." He lamented that "the subject has often been confused with social and political issues of racial inferiority, desegregation, civil rights and other extraneous matters" (Garrett, in Shuey, 1966: vii).

Yet, in the same year, 500,000 copies of a pamphlet bearing his name, with the innocuous title "How Classroom Desegregation Will Work," were distributed to teachers across the country by the Patrick Henry Press, a small publisher of anticommunist literature. In it, Garrett attempted to prove that blacks are biologically inferior to whites, and that race mixing in schools leads to lowered academic standards, higher costs, frustration, absenteeism, intermarriage, delinquency, and ultimately military weakness. Denying he was a racist and a hatemonger, Garrett stated:

> Those black Africans are fine muscular animals when they're not diseased . . . and I think they're fine when they're not frustrated. But when they're frustrated, they revert to primitive savages [Garrett, quoted in Newsweek, 1966: 63].

In another Patrick Henry Press tract appearing that year, entitled "Breeding Down," Garrett endorsed laws that banned marriages between people who were feebleminded, insane, or of different races:

> You can no more mix the two races and maintain the standards of white civilization than you can add 80 (the average IQ of Negroes) and 100 (the average IQ of whites), divide by two and get 100. What you would get would be a race of 90's and it is that 10 percent differential that spells the difference between a spire and a mud hut; 10 percent—or less—is the margin of civilization's profit; it is the difference between a cultured society and savagery. [Garrett, quoted in Karier, 1972: 347-348].

In an interview in which he defended segregated schooling on educational grounds, social scientist Van Den Haag (1964: 1059) criticized the proponents of no innate differences:

> they obstinately refuse to act as scientists, being committed to various causes more than to the cause of science, although they yearn passionately for the trappings and prestige of science. Yet for scientists moderation in the pursuit of truth is a fatal vice; it cannot be offset by extremism in the pursuit of egalitarian ideologies.

In 1965, engineer and Nobel Prize winner in physics Shockley was asked whether the quality of the human race was declining in general and, specifically, to what extent heredity might be responsible for the "high incidence of Negroes on crime and relief rolls." He told the interviewer:

> This is a difficult question to answer. Crime seems to be mildly hereditary, but there is a strong environmental factor. . . . We lack proper scientific investigations, possibly because nobody wants to raise the question for fear of being called a racist. . . . Actually, what I worry about with whites and Negroes alike is this: Is there an imbalance in the reproduction of inferior and superior strains? . . . Warnings about this were heard 100 years ago, but it is still as touchy a subject today as it was then. . . . But the whole subject is being swept under the rug so we have no real facts on the situation. [Shockley, quoted in U.S. News and World Report, 1965: 70].

Shuey (1966: 1, 521) compiled the "ever growing literature" on the subject of Negro intelligence. It would be good to "knock the props from under old prejudices," Shuey wrote, but scientists must proceed without wishful thinking and without awe of prevailing opinion, "whether it be found in the courts, in the pulpit or in the press." Although averring that "the purpose of the book was not to prove that Negroes are socially, morally, or intellectually inferior," Shuey concluded over 500 pages later that native differences in intelligence did indeed exist.

At the University of California in Berkeley, Jensen (1970: 124-125) urged that racial differences can and should be studied. He recommended "no holds barred" research into what has been for decades an ideological battlefield. He charged that the reluctance of scientists to come to grips with the race and IQ issue manifested itself in a number of tendencies: to remain on remote fringes of the subject and sidestep or blur central concerns; to tolerate unusually vague definitions, concepts, and inferences; to demand that practically impossible criteria be met; to deny or belittle widely known facts; to challenge well-established quantitative methods; and to set up straw men and beat dead horses. These tendencies would not be overcome, he predicted, until some of the taboos surrounding research and public discussion of the issue withered away.

Jensen (1973) demanded that attention be paid to the "black IQ deficit" which amounted to roughly one standard deviation below the white average. This 15-point gap between group means resulted in a mental retardation rate (defined as below 70 IQ) for blacks that was seven times greater than for whites. Jensen argued that a scientific theory which frankly recognized genetically determined mental and behavioral differences between the races was 'not a racist theory any more than one that identified inherent physical characteristics. He lamented the emotional furor that greeted his views among social scientists and on campuses because his careful and dispassionate research was intended to stimulate rational discourse and balanced inquiries into a problem that could not be wished away. He insisted that scientists ask tough questions, face the facts, and dispel cherished myths that harmonized so well with a democratic belief in human equality. All reasonable hypotheses must be subjected to rigorous testing, he urged, even those that are "academically and socially taboo."

Something had to be done, Jensen believed, because the educationally and occupationally least able among blacks had a higher reproductive rate than their white counterparts, while the most able stratum of the black community had a lower birth rate than its white counterpart. This "dysgenic" trend could widen the gap in average intelligence between the races over the generations. The superficial dismissal of this intensifying problem by well-meaning wishful thinkers might be viewed in the future as a terrible injustice to black Americans (Jensen, 1970: 131).

The race and IQ issue was not yet resolved, argued Harvard's Herrnstein (1971), and the fundamental question was whether inquiry would once again be shut off because some people believe society is best left in ignorance. He called for more research, not less, since it is necessary to cope with what people are really like rather than the fictions embodied in one political philosophy or another. Harvard bacteriologist Davis wrote in a letter to the president of the National Academy of Sciences that "human races surely differ, to some degree, in the distribution of human potential. . . . It would indeed be tragic if studies were inhibited for fear they might demonstrate some degree of difference" (quoted in Fincher, 1976: 241).

The editor of the conservative journal *National Review,* Buckley (1969: 350), summarized Jensen's findings as "the average Negro is less 'intelligent' than the average white, bluntly put." He contended that although all men are equal from a Christian standpoint, "it will take time to undo the damage brought by the ideologization of science during the reign of American liberalism."

As the egalitarian upsurge of the late 1960s faded in the early 1970s, a virulent backlash against it congealed. Passionate charges of research taboos resounded through the halls of academia and were echoed by allies in scientific, professional, and political circles. The vague innuendoes about a liberal establishment's conspiracy of silence gave way to strident calls for a crackdown against a new "enemy" that was allegedly seeking to enforce a taboo and punish all who defied it: the antiestablishment radical student movement.

The first major attack came in the form of an editorial in the New York Times (1968: 46), lashing out against the "campus totalitarians" of the New Left who had launched militant campaigns to combat the acceptance and spread of Jensen's viewpoint:

> The subjugation of science—including theories of heredity—to the orthodoxies of political revolutions has been the mark of Fascist, Nazi and Stalinist totalitarianism. Surrender to such tactics cannot be tolerated on the American campus.

As reports of demonstrations, picketing, shouting matches, and disruptions filled the press, British IQ expert Eysenck (1972) blasted the "left-fascism" of the student movement:

> Of course any putative differences are due to environmental factors. And of course, anyone who dares to doubt these truths must be a racist, seduced by the establishment into utter intellectual prostitution. . . . And to be sure, if we know the truth . . . then the end justifies the means: burn books, boycott publishers and book sellers, break up meetings, threaten and persecute those who dare disagree with you.

Fifty scientists signed a resolution submitted to the American Psychological Association (1972) that called for unencumbered research into the role of heredity in important behaviors. The statement noted that all through history researchers and teachers have been suppressed by religious and political authorities, and cited several celebrated cases: Galileo in orthodox Italy; Darwin in Victorian England; Einstein in Nazi Germany; and Mendelians during the reign of Lysenkoism in Stalinist Russia. The signatories complained that advocates of hereditarian views were personally abused and their positions misrepresented by emotional and unscientific adversaries. Leftist students called them "fascists." They appealed to a silent majority of scientists to come to the defense of heretics, to vigorously defend the right—even the duty—of scholars to discuss the biological bases of behavior, to deplore the evasion of genetics in contemporary social science textbooks and courses, and to rally faculty, professional, and learned societies to protect vigilantly those who espouse biobehavioral theories.

THE CONTROVERSY RETURNS TO CRIMINOLOGY

In the mid 1970s, the furor about "research taboos" died down in psychology and sociology. But shortly thereafter the issue was born again, this time within criminological circles. The charges were muted and the racial aspects were obscured, but the main thesis retained its familiar thrust: that a powerful group covered up the truth through behind-the-scenes manipulations.

Hirschi and Hindelang (1977: 571-587) called attention to the tendency of criminologists to deemphasize individual differences as non or even antisociological. Among the many possible distinguishing characteristics between delinquents and nondelinquents, none is apparently more threatening to the integrity of sociological criminology and its moral commitments than variations in intelligence, they remarked. Many textbooks did not even mention IQ as an explanatory factor, and most that did denied its significance. Yet the available data suggested to them that IQ scores were as important a predictor of official delinquency as social class or race. Although most modern theorists assumed or explicitly stated that intelligence affected delinquency (through school performance and adjustment), their views were ignored by researchers. Hirschi and Hindelang warned that ignoring IQ differences would continue to restrict and even embarrass sociological criminology. In particular, there was a paucity of appropriately analyzed data about IQ, race, and official delinquency.

The biosocial approach which emphasizes individual differences and the role of genetics received a new impetus and respectability from the recent work of C. Ray Jeffery. While president of the American Society of Criminology, Jeffery (1978) called for a new criminology built on a foundation of biochemistry, psychobiology, sociobiology, and the premise that behavior is determined by both genetics and environmental variables. He proposed that new explanations be sought by courageous researchers. Heading his list of emerging issues was the role of intelligence in criminality. Jeffery pointed to links between low intelligence and delinquency, between XYY abnormalities and low intelligence, and between poverty and inadequate nutrition and low intelligence. Intelligence was related to both genetics and environment but was not directly inheritable. What was genetic, Jeffery contended, was a capacity for interaction with the environment.

Gordon (1976: 265, 270) has observed that only three attempts to explain the crime rate differential between blacks and whites in terms of IQ have appeared in the professional literature recently—his own, Shockley's, and Hirschi's. He expressed the hope that a greater awareness of the suffering due to crime would encourage the adoption of a "more constructive" attitude toward the race and genetics issue. But in his chapter for this book, Gordon reports that he encountered difficulties in locating a journal that would accept his article, due to controversial findings based on race-specific prevalence rates drawn from official delinquency records.

THE REALITY AND THE APPROPRIATE RESPONSE

Despite many charges to the contrary made over the past four decades, the reality is that there are no suppressed truths, no conspiracies of silence, no coverups, and no powerful groups protecting the interests of low IQ individuals, racial minorities, delinquents, or criminals. A prohibition against research into racial differences in intelligence or crime rates has never been implemented, and never could be. The metaphor of taboo is without justification when applied to this scientific controversy.

On a number of occasions, scientists have felt compelled to respond to what they perceived as particularly widely publicized accusations and distortions. However, professional organizations have repeatedly refused to declare any subjects "off limits" to researchers. The typical reply has been to criticize what they viewed as irresponsible statements and refute alleged falsifications, while at the same time holding open the possibility that new evidence would lead to different conclusions. Relevant passages (with emphasis added) from official resolutions appear in Chart 1. The first three excerpts (see Benedict, 1940: 195-199) are from statements issued in response to the racial doctrines of European fascists and American eugenicists. The second set of three excerpts is drawn from replies to Garrett's charges (see Pettigrew, 1964: 134-135). The excerpt from the National Academy of Sciences (1967) was part of a reply to those—especially Shockley—who were insisting on a major shift in research priorities. The last two excerpts are taken from reactions to Jensen's articles (SPSSI, 1969; Rice, 1973). In every case, the phrases "preponderance of scientific opinion," "overwhelming evidence," "no scientific support," "no valid basis," or "little or no ground" invite—perhaps incite—researchers convinced of the existence of significant racial differences in intelligence to go back out into the field, return to the laboratory, and resume their crusade under the banners of the "search for the truth," the "right to open inquiry," and the "freedom to proclaim" scientific views.

The reason why it might appear to some observers that certain subjects are tabooed was succinctly explained by the Council of the National Academy of Sciences (1967) in its statement in response to Shockley's call for new research into racial differences:

> It is indeed possible that some studies have not been carried out for fear that the results might not be acceptable to some groups. Many researchers prefer to work in non-controversial areas where public feelings are not involved and where they can work undisturbed. There is, however, a more valid reason that might keep scientists from working in such areas as the separation of hereditary and environmental contributions to complex human behavioral traits and to racial differences in these traits. This is the conviction that none of the current methods can produce unambiguous results. To shy away from seeking the truth is one thing; to refrain from collecting still more data that would be of uncertain meaning but would invite misuse is another.

In essence, the NAS Council was expounding the doctrine of the social responsibility of scientists that first emerged during the genetics and eugenics battles of the 1930s.

TABLE 1. Excerpts From Official Resolutions By Professional Societies

Organization and Date	Statement (with emphasis added)
American Anthropological Association, 1938	Whereas the prime requisites for science are the honest and unbiased *search for truth and the freedom to proclaim* such truth when discovered and known; and whereas anthropology in many countries is being conscripted and its data distorted and misinterpreted to serve the cause of an unscientific racialism rather than the cause of truth; be it resolved that the American Anthropological Association repudiates such racialism and adheres to the following statement of facts . . . (3) Anthropology provides *no scientific basis* for discrimination against any people on the ground of racial inferiority, religious affiliation or linguistic heritage.
Biologists' Manifesto, Seventh International Genetics Congress, 1939	In the first place, there can be *no valid basis for estimating and comparing* the intrinsic worth of different individuals *without* economic and social conditions which provide approximately *equal* opportunities for all members of society instead of stratifying them from birth into classes with widely different privileges.
Executive Council, SPSSI, American Psychological Association, 1938	In the scientific investigation of human groups by psychologists *no conclusive evidence* has been found for racial or national differences in native intelligence and inherited personality characteristics. Certainly, no individual should be treated as an inferior merely because of his membership in one human group rather than another.
SPSSI, American Psychological Association, 1961	There are differences in intelligence test scores when one compares a random sample of whites and Negroes. What is equally clear is that *no evidence exists* that leads to the conclusion that such differences are innate. Quite to the contrary, the *evidence overwhelmingly* points to the fact that when one compares Negroes and whites of comparable cultural and educational background, differences in intelligence diminish markedly.
SSSP, American Sociological Association, 1961	. . . the *great preponderance of scientific opinion* has favored the conclusion that there is *little or no ground* on which to assume that the racial groups in question are innately different in any important human capacity.
American Anthropological Association, 1961	The AAA repudiates statements now appearing in the United States that Negroes are biologically and in innate mental ability inferior to whites, and reaffirms the fact that there is *no scientifically established evidence* to justify the exclusion of any race from the rights guaranteed by the Constitution of the United States.
Council, National Academy of Sciences, 1967	Despite the great number of tests that have been performed on Negro and white populations, *it is still not clear* whether any differences found are primarily genetic or environmental . . . no promising new approach to answering these questions should be discouraged. While existing methods offer little hope for unambiguous answers, *there is always the possibility* that new insights will come from an unexpected direction. The history of scientific discovery suggests that the best strategy would be the support of basic research from which such insights may arise.

Continued on next page

TABLE 1. (continued)

Organization and Date	Statement (with emphasis added)
SPSSI, American Psychological Association, 1969	As behavioral scientists, we believe that statements specifying the hereditary components of intelligence are *unwarranted by the present state of scientific knowledge* . . . (and) such statements may be seriously misinterpreted, particularly in their applications to social policy . . . The Council of the Society for the Psychological Study of Social Issues reaffirms its long-held position of *support for open inquiry* on all aspects of human behavior. We are concerned with establishing high standards of scientific inquiry and of scientific responsibility.
American Anthropological Association, 1971	. . . condemns as dangerous and unscientific the racist, sexist or anti-working class theories of genetic inferiority propagated by Richard Herrnstein, William Shockley, and Arthur Jensen . . . the irresponsible support of *unfounded conclusions* by the Atlantic Monthly, Harvard Educational Review, and the New York Times.

Appeals to conscience and to social responsibility in the case of IQ and race have been elaborated and extended by other scientists.

Chomsky (1972) argued that the scientist has a clear moral responsibility to show that the importance of his work outweighs any anticipated malicious consequences. What needed to be explained, he asserted, was the zeal and perseverance with which some researchers investigated trivial yet socially explosive issues. The conflict of values—scientific curiosity versus social impact—did not lead to a dilemma, but vanished in this case when it was recognized that any connection between IQ and race had no more scientific significance than a tie between IQ and height, and no social importance except in a racist society where people are treated as members of a group rather than as individuals.

Block and Dworkin (1976: 95-98) proposed a set of criteria to guide scientists in their choice of research topics: If the results are ambiguous and are likely to be distorted by the media in the direction of producing harmful consequences, if the possibilities of countering these misinterpretations are minimal, if the findings are likely to be used selectively to justify the political positions of the powerful and thus the social benefits are small and the costs grave, then the scientist has the responsibility to cease such investigations as long as the above conditions obtain. They do not suggest that since some researchers will reject these standards and continue their work, a second best solution is to counterbalance one-sided designs with alternative models. If environmentalists study the IQ and race issue, they will implicitly endorse the supposed importance of this research. Therefore, they urged that at this time in this country, given the prevailing social and political climate, individual scientists should refrain from inquiring about racial differences. Those who plow ahead oblivious to these appeals act irresponsibly, but coercion must not be used to interfere with their teaching, research, or public appearances.

Not only do social scientists have responsibilities; the subjects of their studies have rights. Research projects exploring the alleged inferiority of entire groups raise this issue in its most dramatic context.

Sagarin (1973) argued that powerless and highly vulnerable groups have a right not to be researched and to tell social scientists to "keep out." The concept of knowledge for its own sake under any and all circumstances must be rejected. Scientists often find that they are compelled to choose sides when they study a group locked in conflict with its opponent. Although basic abstract research might be innocent of responsibility for its uses and consequences, applied social research explicitly attempts to solve practical problems (defined by the dominant group) through social engineering. Hence, scientists conducting agency-funded research into pragmatic issues are acting in a partisan fashion, whether or not they realize their impact. If a group is the object of intense discrimination, sympathetic researchers should understand that their intervention might be perceived as threatening, regardless of their own personal values.

Yet attempts to document the inferiority of nonwhites continue. Appeals to conscience and social responsibility do not deter some scientists or convince them that a research moratorium on racial differences would be justified at this time. Evidently, their consciences are clear. Either they sincerely fancy themselves unbiased observers and nonpartisan seekers of truth, or they reject the arguments about fueling racism and discrimination. By their definitions and ideologies, they are acting responsibly. The concept of social responsibility, like those of "morality," "national security," and the "public interest," obviously can mean different things to different people. Therefore, some people who feel very strongly that research into racial differences in intelligence or crime rates should be discouraged have advocated more severe measures. Rather than appealing to the scientists to choose another subject, or to the disadvantaged groups not to cooperate, they have appealed to the authorities to suppress the basic data.

The IQ test has been under fire for decades because it provides a pretext for effectively segregating school children by race and social class from a very early age. Recently, minority group parents and their allies won an important victory in their struggle against tracking and low-quality schooling. In October 1979, a federal court judge in California declared the use of unvalidated IQ tests as a basis for placement in remedial classes unconstitutional. The court concluded that educators have too often been able to rationalize inaction by blaming failure in ghetto schools on the assumed intellectual inferiority of disproportionate numbers of minority students (Schreier, 1979: 7). This ruling does not halt IQ testing or the administration of similar exams, but it does represent an instance in which data were denied to decision-makers because of the fundamentally prejudicial nature of that data.

Geis (1965) has argued that official statistics pretend to report the criminal behavior of racial groups but really reflect and perpetuate errors and myths which can be misleading or even viciously malevolent. He proposed that racial classifications be dropped from statistical reports to eliminate the numerical fuel which fires prejudice. Minority groups have sound historical reasons to believe that something invidious is intended when racial distinctions are noted in official records. Information about arrests rates by religion and by political affiliation is not maintained, although it might provide data of some explanatory value. In gathering census data, the government has declined to ask certain questions on the ground that there are considerations of greater sensitivity than the needs and interests of social scientists.

However, Radzinowicz and King (1977) urged the opposite course of action. They contend that in England, criminologists, administrators, and the general public would be better served if the national and ethnic origins of both offenders and victims were tabulated, along with sex and age, as they are in the United States. But the British still reject the practice as a form of improper discrimination, a hindrance rather than a help in achieving the integration of immigrants into the mainstream of society. They note that in South Africa, with its policy of strict apartheid, there are no such inhibitions about race-related statistics.

Gordon (1976: 202) has decried the spotty discontinuation of crime statistics by racial categories that has occurred in the United States in recent years. He argues that this suppression of race-related data in official source figures deprives whites of meaningful information about themselves and thereby impedes the progress of social science.

The suppression of race-specific data would be ineffective as an impediment to racism, and it might actually complicate the struggle against racism. In the absence of hard data, superficial impressions or complete conjecture would be used by those intent on giving their prejudices a scientific veneer. The suppression of information would be cited as prime evidence of the existence of a coverup. Worse yet, minority groups and their allies would be deprived of crucial information necessary to document patterns of racial discrimination. Affirmative action goals and timetables require race-related data in order to gauge whether progress is occurring in the rectification of past discrimination. One of the most powerful arguments against the restoration of the death penalty is that it has been and probably will continue to be applied in a discriminatory manner. Specifically, blacks who killed whites were much more likely to be executed than blacks who killed blacks (whites who killed blacks were almost never executed). Information on the race of the offender and of the victim was needed to discern this pattern. As long as discrimination is suspected, race-related statistics must be maintained.

One effective strategy would be to discourage racist research by denying it any funding. Empirical studies using quantitative analysis require costly data-gathering phases and computer time for statistical calculations. But this type of multivariate analysis is precisely the type that readily receives funding from government agencies and private foundations.

Apparently, many scientists feel that the best response to the problem of inflammatory racial studies is to ignore the claims of the researchers. Obviously, it is difficult to determine whether scientists as individuals or in groups are consciously and consistently following a policy of not addressing the accusations of those who complain that the subject is tabooed. The resolution about behavior and heredity circulated among psychologists in 1972 deplored the alleged evasion of genetics in current textbooks and the failure to give credence to biobehavioral outlooks in social science courses. Hirschi and Hindelang reported that many criminology textbooks did not address low IQ as a possible cause of delinquent and criminal behavior.

But the strategy of ignoring provocative race-oriented research has failed, as it must, because the media seeks out the sensational and segregationists search for ammunition. This strategy really backfires when those who claim there is a taboo are able to portray themselves as victims of a conspiracy of silence.

Since Shuey's book about racial differences in intelligence levels (first published in 1958, second edition in 1966) based on 240 studies conducted between 1913 and 1957 forced the issue back into the public spotlight, a steady stream of articles about the continuing debate has appeared. They do not appear in obscure professional journals but in widely read magazines indexed in the Reader's Guide To Periodical Literature. The charges of a coverup have been repeated in leading publications by prominent academic and professional spokesmen. Journalistic accounts of disruptions and scathing editorials denouncing the protesters only heighten interest in the subject. The repeated coverage and wide dissemination of the complaint about a conspiracy of silence is an obvious anomaly. Indeed, the publicity given both to the charges and to those who demonstrate their disdain for the charges ensures that the issue will not fade away in the media, and the continuing intense competition for scarce resources guarantees that races pitted against each other will retain their tensions.

According to a *Time* Magazine article (1979: 49) that provided advance publicity for his then forthcoming book (since published), Jensen was returning to the fray to instigate still another round in the unending battle:

> Jensen's findings clearly have horrendous implications. Indeed, they come close to saying that blacks are a natural and permanent underclass—an idea so shocking that the book is likely to spark the most explosive debate yet over race and IQ.

Shockley has returned to the talk show circuit with his same old message, exploiting the publicity he attracts for his participation in a neoeugenics scheme to impregnate women from Mensa, the high-IQ society, with sperm donated by Nobel Prize winners.

Confrontation is the only viable strategy to combat the resurgence of scientific racism and elitism. The implications and consequences of these ideas for crime control policies must be thoroughly exposed by recalling the lessons of the past. The demands for action that will turn back the clock and revive the worst practices of previous generations must be answered by reasoned debate and all forms of legal, nonviolent pressure tactics. Each occasion provides an opportunity to clarify issues and sharpen struggles which are otherwise fought behind the scenes and couched in code words, technical jargon, and euphemisms. Racist and elitist researchers must be held accountable for playing the historic role of helping to usher in a period of backlash and reaction after an era of progress and enlightenment.

Leftists have been the staunchest advocates and defenders of egalitarian principles and have been in the forefront of efforts to combat those who want to resurrect the fears, prejudices, and discriminatory practices of the dismal past. But the current lull in radical activism provides another opening for backlash views to reemerge.

Race relations in the United States are once again at a crossroad. In his survey of American attitudes, Myrdal (1944:

655, 966) noted that the crime rate for black people had been the object of statistical measurements since 1890, the subject of recurring biased and sensationalized news reports, and the focus of periodic heated debates. Myrdal observed that "whites believe the Negro to be innately addicted to crime."

Recent public-opinion poll results reveal that the center of gravity has shifted and that an encouraging trend toward enlightenment has emerged, but an ominous tendency persists.

As each row in Table 1 shows, overt expressions of white supremacist beliefs—despite some short-lived resurgences—are on the wane. Diminishing numbers of white people openly admit to the racist stereotypes of the past. Yet a hardcore group of 15 to 25% of respondents still cling to the segregationist tenets that black people are generally inferior and, in particular, are genetically less intelligent. Up to one-third of the white people in these polls automatically associate black people with crime and violence.

What if complaints about research taboos were received with great sympathy by the scientific community and all resistance to racist and elitist ideological onslaughts crumbled? Suppose the allegedly forbidden line of reasoning—that blacks get into trouble with the law more frequently than whites because they are (inherently?) less intelligent, and mentally inferior people are more likely to be criminally inclined than intellectually

TABLE 2. What Whites Believe About Blacks

"Statements sometimes heard"	Percentage of whites who agreed					
	1963	1966	1967	1971	1976	1978
Blacks have less native intelligence than whites	39	36	46	37	28	25
Blacks breed crime	35	33	32	27	31	29
Blacks are more violent than whites	—*	—*	42	36	35	34
Blacks are inferior to white people	31	26	29	22	15	15

*not asked that year

SOURCE: Polls by Louis Harris and Associates for the National Conference of Christians and Jews. (Newsweek, 1979: 48)

superior people—once again shaped mainstream criminological thought and significantly influenced crime control programs. Would public enthusiasm for humanizing prison conditions and guaranteeing inmate rights be heightened? Would public support for greater efforts to crack down on white-collar crime by businessmen and government officials be strengthened? Would changes to reduce the stigmatization that haunts ex-convicts and foils their attempts to "go straight" become more acceptable? What impact would scientifically endorsed (even through silence) beliefs about black intellectual inferiority and criminality have on campaigns to improve opportunities for victims of discrimination and to integrate police forces, the courts, and correctional staffs? Would the number of instances in which white police officers use excessive—and sometimes deadly—force on black suspects decline?

Those who want to push a race-IQ-crime interpretation seek to be interviewed, to be quoted, to write articles and books, to gain recognition, and to influence crime-fighting strategies. They gather together and plan ways to reach a wider audience of scientists and citizens with their message.

Those who oppose them and have alternative explanations for the same reality do what they can to prevent the spread of these doctrines. These counterattacks against racist and elitist offensives and the efforts by humanists, egalitarians, and leftists to fight back and defend their principles and the gains in social justice that have been accomplished should not be confused with unscientific attempts to enforce alleged research taboos.

Political rulers and religious leaders in past centuries did indeed suppress the truth, punish heretics, burn books, and ban ideas. Today, some social scientists—and even some criminologists—are trying to picture themselves as victims of a conspiracy to hide the truth about race, intelligence, and crime. But the analogy is completely false, and claims of these correlations are unfounded unless definitions are carefully tailored to meet the requirements of statistical manipulations.

How could these scientists not expect a forceful and furious reply when they use computers to try to convince the public of essentially the same old message that the cross burners preach?

REFERENCES

ALLEN, G. (1974) "A history of eugenics in the class struggle." Science for the People 6 (March): 26-38.

American Psychological Association (1972) "Behavior and heredity" (resolution of scientists). American Psychologist 27: 660-661.

BENEDICT, R. (1940) Race: Science and Politics. New York: Viking.

BLOCK, N. and G. DWORKIN [eds.] (1976) The IQ Controversy. New York: Pantheon.

BONGER, W. (1943) Race and Crime. Montclair, NJ: Patterson-Smith.

BUCKLEY, W. (1969) "On Negro 'inferiority.' " National Review 2 (April 8): 350.

CHOMSKY, N. (1972) "The fallacy of Richard Herrnstein's IQ." Social Policy (May/June): 19-25.

EMPEY, L. (1978) American Delinquency. St. Paul, MN: West.

EYSENCK, H. (1972) "The dangers of the new zealots." Encounter 34 (December): 79-89.

FINCHER, J. (1976) Human Intelligence. New York: G. P. Putnam.

GARRETT, H. (1961) "One psychologist's view of 'equality of the races.' " U.S. News and World Report 51 (August 14): 72-74.

GEIS, G. (1965) "Statistics concerning race and crime." Crime and Delinquency 11 (April): 142-150.

GORDON, R. (1976) "Prevalence: the rare datum in delinquency measurement and its implications for the theory of delinquency," pp. 201-284 in Malcolm Klein (ed.) The Juvenile Justice System. Beverly Hills, CA: Sage Publications.

HERRNSTEIN, R. (1971) "IQ." Atlantic Monthly (September): 44-64.

HIRSCHI, T. and M. HINDELANG (1977) "Intelligence and delinquency: a revisionist review." Amer. Soc. Rev. 42: 571-587.

HOOTON, E. (1939) Twilight of Man. New York: G. P. Putnam.

INGLE, D. (1961) "Racial differences in mental abilities have not been proven." U.S. News and World Report 51 (August 14): 74.

JEFFERY, C. (1978) "Criminology as an interdisciplinary behavioral science." Criminology 16: 149-169.

JENSEN, A. (1970) "Can we and should we study race differences?" pp. 124-145 in J. Hellmuth (ed.) The Disadvantaged Child, Vol. III. New York: Brunner Mazel.

——— (1973) "The differences are real." Psychology Today 7 (December): 80-86.

KARIER, C. (1972) "Testing for order and control in the corporate liberal state." Educ. Theory 22 (Spring): 154-180.

KORN, R. and L. McCORKLE (1959) Criminology and Penology. New York: Holt, Rinehart & Winston.

LUDMERER, K. (1972) Genetics and American Society. Baltimore: Johns Hopkins Univ. Press.

McGURK, F. (1956) "A scientist's report on race differences." U.S. News and World Report 41 (September 21): 92-95.

MONTAGU, A. (1975) Race and I.Q. New York: Oxford Univ. Press.

MURCHISON, C. (1926) Criminal Intelligence. Worcester, MA: Clark Univ. Press.

MYRDAL, G. (1944) An American Dilemma. New York: Harper & Row.

National Academy of Sciences (1967) Council. "Racial studies: academy states position on call for new research." Science 158: 892-893.

Newsweek (1966) "Lesson in bias." 67 (May 30): 63.

——— (1979) "A new racial poll." 93 (February 26): 48.

New York Times (1968) "Campus totalitarians" (editorial). (May 20): 46.

PETTIGREW, T. (1964) A Profile of the Negro American. New York: Litton.

PLATT, A. (1974) "The triumph of benevolence," pp. 356-389 in R. Quinney (ed.) Criminal Justice in America: A Critical Understanding. Boston: Little, Brown.

PUTNAM, C. (1961) Race and Reason: A Yankee View. Washington, DC: Public Affairs Press.

QUINNEY, R. (1979) Criminology. Boston: Little, Brown.

——— and J. WILDEMAN (1977) The Problem of Crime. New York: Harper & Row.

RADZINOWICZ, L. and J. KING (1977) The Growth of Crime. New York: Basic Books.

RENNIE, J. (1978) The Search For Criminal Man. Lexington, MA: D. C. Heath.

RICE, B. (1973) "The high cost of thinking the unthinkable." Psychology Today 7 (December): 89-93.

SAGARIN, E. (1967) "Race and crime: a revisit to an old concept." Delivered at the meeting of the American Society of Criminology, Washington, DC.

——— (1973) "The research setting and the right not to be researched." Social Problems 21: 52-64.

SCHLAPP, M. and E. SMITH (1928) The New Criminology. New York: Boni and Liveright.

SCHREIER, H. (1979) "California judge rules IQ test unconstitutional." In These Times 3 (November 14-20): 7.

SENNA, C. (1973) The Fallacy of IQ. New York: Third Press.

SHELDON, W. (1949) Varieties of Delinquent Youth. New York: Harper & Row.

SHUEY, A. (1966) The Testing of Negro Intelligence. New York: Social Science Press.

Society for the Psychological Study of Social Issues (1969) "The SPSSI statement." Harvard Educ. Rev. 39 (Summer): 625-27.

SUTHERLAND, E. (1931) "Mental deficiency and crime," in K. Young (ed.) Social Attitudes. New York: Holt, Rinehart & Winston.

Time (1979) "The return of Arthur Jensen." (September 24): 49.

TULCHIN, S. (1939) Intelligence and Crime. Chicago: Univ. of Chicago Press.

U.S. News and World Report (1965) "Is the quality of U.S. population declining? Interview with a Nobel prize-winning scientist." 59 (November 22): 68-70.

VAN DEN HAAG, E. (1964) "Intelligence or prejudice?" National Review 16 (December 1): 1057-1059.

VOLD, G. (1979) Theoretical Criminology. New York: Oxford Univ. Press.

WEYL, N. (1973) "Race, nationality, and crime." Mankind Quarterly 14 (July-September): 41-48.

6

C. Ray Jeffery
Florida State University

SOCIOBIOLOGY AND CRIMINOLOGY:
The Long Lean Years of
the Unthinkable and the Unmentionable

The repression of scientific thought has had a very long history indeed. We can start with the death of Socrates by hemlock. Socrates challenged the basic beliefs of the Greek society of his time; his particular sin was that he believed that correct action implied correct thought. He was sentenced to death for his contention that the rulers of Athens did not know how to rule. If we were to apply the Socratic principle to our society today—that is, if those who thought our rulers did not know how to rule were sentenced as was the Greek philosopher— many of us would be drinking hemlock. Socrates taught that ignorance could not be tolerated, and this was evidence enough to condemn a man to death.

The story of Genesis, of Adam and Eve, contains the idea that man fell from the grace of God and the Garden of Eden when he tasted the apple of knowledge of good and evil. Because of the sin of knowledge, Adam was sentenced to work for a living and Eve to bear children in pain. From this fall from Eden, we now have creeping socialism and the feminist movement.

The clash between orthodoxy and science is no better illustrated than by the conflict between the Catholic Church and Galileo. Galileo was persecuted for his work in astronomy and his support of the Copernican theory that the earth moves around the sun. At that time, the dispute over whether the earth was flat or round was also a major issue. Galileo was forced to recant his teachings about astronomy. It is ironic that Galileo died in 1642, the year in which Isaac Newton was born. Some historians of science attribute the shift of the scientific movement from Italy to England to the action of the Catholic Church against Galileo. At any rate, the major developments in science did occur in England, with Isaac Newton, Francis Bacon, and Charles Darwin.

Michael Servetus was burned at the stake by John Calvin for his studies of the circulation of the blood. The Hungarian physician Semmelweis discovered that puerperal fever (childbirth fever) was spread by the attending physicians through their dirty, infected hands and that this deadly plague could be stopped by the simple procedure of physicians washing their hands. For this, Semmelweis was driven to an insane asylum by his contemporaries.

Charles Darwin was widely attacked after the publication of his *Origin of Species* in 1859, culminating in the famous debate between Thomas Huxley and Bishop Wilberforce concerning the role of evolution in human affairs. In the United States, the Scopes trial in 1925 involved a young biology instructor who was accused of teaching the doctrine of evolution. Clarence Darrow represented the defense and William Jennings Bryan the prosecution. We still have state and local laws controlling what can and cannot be taught in the way of biology and genetics.

Gregor Mendel, the Austrian monk, taught that there were units of inheritance called genes which were responsible for the characteristics of plants and animals. In opposition to the Mendelian view of genetics was the Lamarckian theory of acquired characteristics, namely, that those characteristics acquired during life from experience with the environment were passed on to the young. This argument is still found today in psychology, sociology, and biology in the form of genetics versus environment, nature versus nurture, inheritance versus learning.

During the Stalinist era in Russia, T. D. Lysenko, a lowly county agricultural agent, was put in charge of agricultural policy in Russia because of his firm belief in Lamarckian acquired characteristics and his denial of genetics. He put wheat seeds in cold water and planted them in the belief that the seeds would acquire the ability to survive in a cold climate such as that found in Siberia. As a result of this policy, Russia has been buying huge amounts of wheat in recent years from the United States. There was a most prestigious group of geneticists in Russia at the time that Stalin took power, and these geneticists were jailed, exiled, or escaped to other countries such as the United States. They included, among others, T. Dobzhansky and H. J. Muller.

During the 1890-1930 era, another political aspect of genetics came to the fore in the form of racism. The ideas of de Gobineau and Chamberlain on racial differences and racial supremacy were used by Hitler and the Nazis as a basis for human experimentation and the mass extermination of Jews in Germany.

Thus, the development of biology and genetics was in that historic period when communism and fascism were emerging as major political ideologies in Europe and, to a lesser extent, in America. Biology became enshrouded in politics. At the same time, we witnessed the rise of behaviorism as a major school in psychology, with such people as Watson, Thorndike, Hull, Guthrie, Skinner, and other learning theorists. This approach to learning ignored or minimized the role of genetics and the functioning of the central nervous system in learning and placed the emphasis on a Lockean tabula rasa and associationism. This was a pure environmentalist view of behavior, as was communism.

During the twentieth century, there was a total move to environmentalism and a total rejection of the individual as a contributor to his behavior. American psychology and sociology have been dominated by several basic assumptions which make any interdisciplinary approach to behavior impossible. These assumptions include: *environmentalism,* the idea that the dominance of the environment controls behavior through non-physical means and nonphysical processes; *equipotentiality,* the assumption that every individual is capable of the same behaviors—given the same environment—as every other individual; and *dualism,* the belief that the state of nature is bifurcated into mind versus matter, genetics versus environment, innate versus learned, man versus nature, and nature versus nurture. One cannot understand the conflict between biology and sociology without first understanding the basic assumptions that sociologists make about human behavior. Sociologists for the most part assume that behavior is learned in social groups without prior biological limitations or restraints and that whatever behavior is exhibited is a product of social learning. Learning theory as now found in psychology is based on biology. However, sociologists continue to write about learning as if they knew what learning theory is all about (Hilgard and Bower, 1975; Seligman and Hager, 1973).

Early criminology was very biological in orientation, due to the impact of Darwin and Lombroso on the discipline. Textbooks on criminology were Lombrosian in nature, as seen in the foreword to MacDonald's book, written in 1893, in which Lombroso wrote that "our school has taken deep root in America" (Hall, 1945: 345). The works of Drähms and Parson were heavily in debt to the ideas of the biologists. In 1924, Sutherland, fresh from the University of Chicago and the psychological school of symbolic interactionists, published the first edition of his famous text, in which he made only passing references to Lombroso, and those in a very negative way. Sutherland based his work largely on W. I. Thomas and his definition of the situation, and he totally rejected any contribution from psychology or biology to criminology. Criminology came to be dominated by Sutherland as a result of this textbook and his other contributions, such as his work on white-collar crime. The text, which is still in existence (Sutherland and Cressey, 1974), rejects psychology and biology. In the 1974 edition, Cressey states that "heredity has not been demonstrated to have any connection whatsoever with criminal behavior." He cites as proof a reference to a 1949 article. But modern genetics did not get under way until 1954, and the behavioral genetics and psychobiology of today is not what it was even ten years ago.

A major revolution occurred in biology after 1954 as a result of the joining of biology and chemistry, and particularly, the work of Watson and Crick. From biochemistry, biology joined psychology in the form of psychobiology and behavioral genetics. Today, psychology is well grounded in biology, as can be seen in introductory textbooks which devote one-third to one-half of the text to the biological bases of behavior. The latest interdisciplinary field to emerge is sociobiology, with the publication of E. O. Wilson's *Sociobiology* in 1975. Since then, several major books and journal articles have appeared devoted to sociobiology, including *Man in Society* by Pierre van den Berghe, a sociologist. Most of the work in this area, however, is being conducted by biologists and ethologists.

Sociobiology set off a great debate, due primarily to the extreme left. The communist ideology of anti-positivism, anti-bourgeoisism, radical sociology/criminology, and historical materialism is gravely challenged by any notion of the biological foundations of behavior. The Science for the People movement at Harvard and MIT attacked Wilson both physically and intellectually, and the man suffered from many personal assaults (Caplan, 1978).

In 1978, I was in the Netherlands as a Fulbright-Hays scholar, and while there I observed the development of a biological program in criminology at the University of Leiden under Wouter Buikhuisen. Buikhuisen is attempting to establish an interdisciplinary program in criminology, and he has added four biologists to the staff of the Institute of Criminology. He has also participated in an interdisciplinary workshop in criminology involving biologists, psychologists, and sociologists. A research project is now under way in Israel involving Shoham, Mednick, Rubin, and Buikhuisen. This project is divided into four subtopics: social, neurophysiological, psychobiological, and endocrinological. If it is allowed to develop, this may become one of the most significant research projects of the future.

Buikhuisen was subject to intensive criticism and investigation from the Parliament, and he was criticized by criminologists and sociologists for reintroducing Naziism into the Netherlands. The Dutch are still living in the shadow of the Second World War, and they have never recovered psychologically from the Nazi occupation and the Anne Frank story. One has only to cry "Nazi," and all reason disappears. When Professor Buikhuisen was installed as Professor of Criminology at the University of Leiden, he was greeted with tire chains and smoke bombs. Fortunately there was no bloodshed, thanks to the skill with which Buikhuisen controlled the situation. I know of few individuals who are kinder, gentler, or more concerned for their fellowmen than Wouter Buikhuisen, and it was a real experience for me to see a man of his stature attacked so vehemently for espousing modern genetics and modern psychology. Nothing he said could not be found in any basic psychology or biology textbook in the United States.

As President of the American Society of Criminology, I established as the theme for the 1978 annual meeting in Dallas, "Criminology: International and Interdisciplinary." I divided the program into biological, psychological, social, and legal/political aspects of criminology. Several invited speakers addressed issues concerning biology, psychology, and crime: Mednick on genetics and crime, Gordon on IQ and crime, Hoffer on the biochemical aspects of crime, Lewis on psychopathology and crime, and Halleck on biological psychiatry and crime. There were a number of sessions devoted to violence and aggression, to new treatment methods, and to new developments in biopolitics. A book is now out composed of papers from the conference (Jeffery, 1979). During the annual banquet, the man honored with the international Sellin-Glueck award took the occasion to attack me and the meeting as a return to "Neo-Lombrosianism." The fact that current work in genetics and biology bears no relationship to the type of biology available to Lombroso did not seem to bother this man, nor did it bother him that the award carried the name of Glueck and that the Gluecks devoted a lifetime at Harvard studying the biological and psychological aspects of criminal behavior. I was also attacked in a Dutch newspaper for bringing controversial topics into the ASC meeting. In a recent article in *Crime and Social Justice,* Platt and Takagi attacked me for not conforming to Marxist principles of historical materialism.

Several biopoliticians who are now exploring the relationship between biology and politics have been bitterly attacked at public meetings as fascists and Nazis, though these men were

Jewish refugees from Nazi Germany who had to flee Naziism in order to survive. This raises the issue of who is qualified to discuss the political foundations of science and research.

The new biology of recent years has rekindled several major issues, for example, the role of biology in sex roles and sex differences, the role of IQ in educational achievement and socioeconomic status, and the role of biological and neurological factors in deviant behavior. Psychiatric treatment has moved from couch therapy to drug therapy. The neurochemical bases of behavior now form a new foundation for psychiatric treatment. The impact of drug therapy is well illustrated by the decline in the number of hospitalized schizophrenics since the introduction of chloropromazine.

One of the leading figures in biopsychiatric research and mental illness is H. M. van Praag of the University of Utrecht. When I was in Holland, I visited van Praag at the University Hospital in Utrecht, and we discussed the recent advances in the diagnosis of schizophrenia and depression and the role of dopamine in these diseases. A few days later, I visited the major mental hospital in the Netherlands, the van den Hoeven Clinic in Utrecht. There I found there were no biological treatments available to the patients and that therapy is based on a social-work concept of resocialization and individual responsibility for one's behavior. I was told that the hospital staff dominated by social workers was hostile to biological interpretations of mental illness. Here we have in a single city one of the most advanced research programs in biopsychiatry and the treatment of mental illness and, at the same time, one of the most backward mental hospitals imaginable.

Recently, three major projects have been killed by various anti-research pressures: (1) the Harvard Study of XYY, (2) the UCLA effort to establish a center to study violence, and (3) the behavioral modification programs in the Federal prison system. Research in the area of genetics has been seriously limited in the past, and most research with human subjects is now almost impossible. And let us not forget that the famous report by the late Robert Martinson and his associates (Lipton et al., 1975) was suppressed by the State of New York before legal action forced its release.

While discussing the censorship of new ideas and the punishment of those who espouse them, one should emphasize that it is not always the state or church that resorts to such tactics. Most of the examples I have used involve church or state, but we must remember that according to Kuhn's analysis of scientific revolutions (Kuhn, 1962), major paradigms are developed and defended by academic disciplines and by the professors who work within academic disciplines. Each academic discipline has a major paradigm or two which governs what is published and what is taught. Within the academic community, these paradigms are reinforced and maintained by academicians in positions of power in order to publish articles, to hire faculty, or to change curriculum content or graduate training. Publications are carefully channeled into very narrow molds, so individuals must write to please the paradigm or go unpublished. This is accomplished by a peer review board which remains anonymous and which can cut the heart out of any new idea. This is guaranteed to produce mediocrity. While I was editor of *Criminology,* I did not use peer review panels on the ground that they would reduce the quality of articles to such a level that no one could be insulted nor challenged. I wanted the liberty to publish controversial articles, even articles I disagreed with, and I wanted to take the responsibility for such articles. I also wanted to give others an opportunity to respond to such articles. This does not usually happen under the peer review system. When several psychologists challenged the basic correctness of Skinnerian psychology, a reviewer commented, "These results are no more likely than shit in a cuckoo clock" (Seligman and Hager, 1973: 15). Later on, the editor of a psychology journal apologized to Garcia for the rejection of his articles.

We should be aware of the fact that the academic community is not committed to the pursuit of truth, but rather to the preservation of ideology. Professors, like lawyers, have designed a system by which truth emerges only by accident and after a terrible struggle. Individuals involved in the pursuit of new ideas are punished for these transgressions, and those who preach orthodoxy are rewarded. It would be simple to show how, through reward and punishment, graduate students are shaped and molded in a system that is supported by hiring and firing practices, academic tenure, the prestige of academic institutions, and other related variables.

The rejection of new ideas is itself not new. If we examine some of the justifications given for such censorship, however, we find only the most humanitarian reasons cited. The current effort to oppose sociobiology is generally placed within the context of protecting the criminal from cruel and unusual punishments. Under the logic of the criminal law and the American system of justice, an individual can be placed in a cell for a long period of time or executed, but we cannot rehabilitate him. We oppose medical care for inmates, but we do not oppose the brutality of our present criminal justice system. We view psychosurgery, genetic counseling, and drug therapy as too dangerous to use. As I have argued elsewhere, a system of treatment demands a therapeutic bill of rights, as Kittrie called it, and it demands that we act responsibly and professionally in our treatment roles.

We probably know less about the human brain and human behavior than most other topics. If we are willing to tolerate such ignorance, we must be willing to pay a high price in terms of poverty, crime, mental illness, and suicide. We have governmental programs for reducing poverty and crime, improving the educational or economic level of the poor, and reducing warfare or pollution, but we enter into such policies without the slightest idea of what we are doing. It is time to face the high cost of our ignorance about the human animal.

REFERENCES

CAPLAN, A. L. (1978) The Sociobiology Debate. New York: Harper & Row.

HALL, J. (1945) "Criminology," in G. Gurvitch and W. Moore (eds.) Twentieth Century Sociology. New York: Philosophical Library.

HILGARD, E. and G. BOWER (1975) Theories of Learning. Englewood Cliffs, NJ: Prentice-Hall.

JEFFERY, C. R. (1979) Biology and Crime. Beverly Hills, CA: Sage Publications.

KUHN, T. (1962) The Structure of Scientific Revolutions. Chicago: Univ. of Chicago Press.

LIPTON, D., R. MARTINSON, and J. WILKS (1975) The Effectiveness of Correctional Treatment. New York: Praeger.

SELIGMAN, M.E.P. and J. HAGER (1973) Biological Boundaries of Learning. Englewood Cliffs, NJ: Prentice-Hall.

SUTHERLAND, E. H. and D. R. CRESSEY (1974) Criminology. Philadelphia, PA: J. B. Lippincott.

7

REPLIES, REBUTTALS, REJOINDERS, RIPOSTES, RETORTS, AND REPARTEE

Michael Levin replies:

I trust that Gordon will do the necessary work of pointing out the fallacies, non sequiturs, and abuses of language which Karmen apparently mistakes for argument. I will confine myself to some general remarks about the significance of the issue at hand and the position which Karmen and (to some extent) Sagarin represent. It is hard to tell if Karmen actually does dissent from the principle of unlimited inquiry. He evidently eschews legislation against research into the links between race, intelligence, and crime, but only because such legislation would be ineffective and, perish the thought, might hinder "affirmative action." However, he does recommend the display of anger as an appropriate response to dissent from environmentalist orthodoxy. Since, as I stressed, intellectual freedom is as much a matter of the climate of scientific opinion as it is of legal constraints, I have to count him as opposed to unlimited inquiry.

I hope I am not reading too much into his essay when I locate him somewhere on the political Left. I mention this so as to heed Sagarin's suggestion that we look at current social reality instead of Millsian utopias. For when we do, what do we see? Is it the fascist Right that is designing social policy with dogmas, issuing bureaucratic ukases, and quashing dissent with demagogy and force? Hardly. Find a demonstration against a speaker, a ransacked office, or fever-pitch emotion directed against hypothesis, and you find the Left. Precisely where are the reactionaries who would return us to phrenology and *The Myth of the Twentieth Century* that the Left is protecting us from? Jensen's *Bias in Mental Testing* is a model of cool reasonableness. Herrnstein never tires of stressing that the last thing the Nazis would have wanted is a genuinely scientific testing of their racial ideas, if only because their brand of frenzy is incompatible with objectivity. Again (and again and again) what is at issue is not the morality of particular experimental procedures—as Sagarin seems to think—but the morality of pursuing certain questions by means which are otherwise morally acceptable.

With the exception of the years 1932-1945, it has been the Left which has been the most strident foe of scientific objectivity in the present century. This is so, I suspect, because of several related doctrines. The first is a passionate environmentalism inherited no doubt from Marx, who seems never to have appreciated the lessons of his contemporary Darwin. This would be harmless, were it not backed up by the conviction that there are no objective facts about social reality, or that, if there are, they are inaccessible to scientific methods. To the Marxist, then, the attempt to discern whether environmentalism is *true* is wholly misguided. Good guys are environmentalists (who will perhaps *make* environmentalism true by letting their belief determine their praxis); the rest of us are mired in sin. This is even clearer when feminists take the stage; their visceral certainty that *all* gender differences are socially determined can only arise from a wholesale repudiation of reality. Needless to say, this is all nonsense; the extent of truth in environmentalism is an objective matter about which we can make well-supported guesses. And perhaps this is the place to roast that chestnut about IQ being a scientifically disreputable concept. IQ is an explication of the ordinary concept of intelligence in just the way the physicist's "force" regiments a good ordinary concept. People clearly do mean something definite by "intelligent": witness our incomprehension at someone who seriously asserts that Gauss was not intelligent. But if "intelligence" raises hackles, we can drop it and call IQ tests "KQ tests." What matters is how well performance on such tests—whatever we call them—

correlates with other variables such as performance in college. Such correlations supply the empirical significance of IQ or KQ tests, and their existence naturally invites physiological and, ultimately, genetic-biological speculation about their basis in human organisms. Doubtless, tests can be devised on which black children will outperform white; a test given in "Black English" will almost surely have this result. What needs showing and never gets it is a correlation between high scores on such tests and competence at other tasks, socially desirable or not.

But the most deeply entrenched dogma of the frenzied Left is the conviction that norms and policy can and should be decided *in advance* of empirical inquiry. This is virtually a corollary of the doubts of leftists about the possibility of value-free science. Thus, we should make a decision about women in the armed forces *before* finding out the effects of this policy on discipline, since any survey of effects will simply reflect the surveyor's biases. Surely, however, a more reasonable approach to questions of social policy (if not to questions of "ultimate" values) is to uncover the pertinent data first, and to ask whether our policies actually serve the ends they were designed to secure.

The uninterrupted expansion of modern science over the last three centuries tempts us to think that this flourishing is inevitable and permanent, and hence that debates like this one are academic. Science will not crumble if Jensen is shouted down or publication denied to anyone who suggests that homosexuality is abnormal, it is asserted. But this is not so. The hegemony of science is very fragile. Science arose only because an unimaginably complex constellation of factors were just right. Had the Persians won at Marathon or Islam at Tours, the discoveries of Galileo, Newton, and Hertz would probably not have been made. Perhaps if Russia gains de facto control of the world, and no longer feels the need to prove herself the equal of the West in point of a now defunct scientific establishment, the world will slide into a new Dark Age made more tenebrous by presently existing technology. The price of intellectual liberty, just as much as political liberty, is eternal vigilance. Challenges to the principle of unlimited inquiry should not be taken or dismissed lightly.

Andrew Karmen replies:

The fundamental premise which underlies this discussion on taboos in criminology is that it would be no exaggeration to concede that certain subjects are just about "off limits" to researchers. At first, I accepted this premise and assumed that a prime example would be the pressures directed against those who sought to establish relationships between race, IQ, and crime. The confrontations between radical students and professors Shockley, Jensen, and Herrnstein immediately came to mind. But as I became immersed in tracing the origin and development of this controversy, I came across so many studies and references that I began to conclude that actually there was no taboo. Only after the consensus crumbled among fledgling social scientists that differences in crime rates between individuals, groups, and entire races could be satisfactorily explained by notions of inferiority/superiority did the charges of taboo, conspiracy, and cover-up arise. The accusations intensified in volume and frequency as the centers of attention of a maturing social science shifted toward other variables.

If the taboo metaphor was greatly overdrawn in the most "clear-cut" case, then I suspected it might be even more inappropriate to so label the resistance to sociobiological and biocriminological revivals and the criticism of claims that feminist victories fed female criminality. I expected that other contributors to this volume would consider it their obligation to furnish hard evidence to support the often heard charges they echoed about intense pressures blocking these lines of inquiry. Instead, they all accepted the premise without question, as if it had been sufficiently documented by previous complainants, and proceeded to fulminate against militant students, feminists, and assorted other leftists. Boiled down to its essence, their argument rests on the belief that elitism, racism, and sexism no longer infect social science, and that minorities and women receive "preferential treatment" from sympathetic or intimidated criminologists. I strongly disagree with the basic themes presented by Levin, Gordon, Henson, and Jeffery, and remain unconvinced of the existence of research taboos in these areas.

Henson never comes to grips with the question she asks at the outset, "Is female crime a taboo topic?" She explains why it should not be, and speculates that feminist leaders exploit attacks on the movement's gains to rekindle the outrage that inspires activism. As for research taboos, she provides no specifics about who, where, when, and how.

Levin also fails to present any data or substantiation. He conjures up hypothetical examples full of Xs, Ys, As, Bs, Es, Rs, and other abstractions tailored to prove his points, but he never comes down from his philosopher's perch to grapple with real people, actual situations, and painful dilemmas.

Both Gordon and Jeffery recite incidents during which prominent exponents of inflammatory outlooks were shouted down and threatened. These events give the argument that research taboos exist an initial plausibility—until it is recalled that complaints of suppression of the truth were voiced for decades, long before any of the campus confrontations materialized. Furthermore, their assessment of the significance of these disruptions differs sharply from the views of the demonstrators themselves. The participants did not think of themselves as potent enforcers of a widely respected taboo, as arms of a scientific establishment, or as defenders of the faith. They sensed they were part of an outgroup, excluded from power, vilified and abused.

Like many others before them, Gordon and Jeffery dropped hints throughout their papers of the existence of an establishment conspiracy that operates behind the scenes to thwart the investigations of those who are not intimidated by the visible deterrents, the demonstrations. Yet, again they fail to bring forth solid proof. Gordon promises at the start to steer a course somewhere between mere gossip and participant observation, but descends to innuendo as his narrative unfolds. His ambiguous data, which consist of comments from journal referees (whom he admits did not explicitly denounce his conclusions about racial differences in delinquency rates), surely lends itself to other, less conspiratorial interpretations. It appears to me that Jeffery, like Gordon, oversimplifies the Kuhnian model to . suit his purposes. In the social sciences, and in criminology in particular, there are continuous theoretical debates and periodic crises, as champions of competing paradigms struggle for hegemony. Surprisingly, Jeffery paints a picture of a monolithic academic establishment that rewards orthodoxy and punishes heresy. Perhaps, as a member of the inner circle, he has documentary proof that sociobiology suffered long lean years as an unthinkable and unmentionable orientation. But the hard data he reviews, including his own impressive accomplishments, undercut his entire argument. How could sociobiology be a tabooed viewpoint when one of its leading and most outspoken advocates was recently elected president of the American Society of Criminology, was a Fulbright-Hays scholar, and previously had been editor of *Criminology*?

What I find intriguing about these four papers is not the weak examples they cite but the strong cases they ignore. Conspiracies and coverups are integral to the notion of research taboos, yet not one of the four contributors who believe taboos do exist, but should not, directed attention to subjects that indisputably are "off limits." I am referring to situations, policies, and programs that are classified—allegedly for our own good—on the ground of national security. In the last decade, courageous journalists, muckrakers, and even some professional criminologists collided with a wall of secrecy as they conducted research into the illegal activities of giant corporations, powerful government agencies, and prominent individuals. In many cases, they were told in no uncertain terms to "keep out" or "keep quiet," or they would have to face the consequences. Insiders who brought the public and researchers firsthand information about illegal activities at home and abroad by the FBI and the CIA, such as Turner, Ellsberg, Marchetti, Agee, Snepp, and Stockwell, have been harassed and punished in various ways. Although a great deal has been written in recent years about official lawlessness, powerful forces are at work to resurrect the taboo and rearm the enforcers. One expression of this counterrevolution against a more open and accountable government is the current attack on the Freedom of Information Act, which has proven itself to be an indispensable research tool for battering down the barriers of unjustifiable secrecy and prying loose vital data.

Why is it that those who decry any obstacle put in the path of criminological research overlook the legal maneuvers by the FBI to keep secret most of its files about the Rosenberg atom spy case and the efforts under J. Edgar Hoover to bar the authors of a book that raised the possibility of a frame-up from airing their views on a TV talk show? How can those who denounce the suppression of basic data forget to mention that many key documents are still classified that deal with the assassination of President Kennedy, Watergate, Koreagate, the CIA's MK-Ultra mind control experiments, and the FBI's illegal counterintelligence program (COINTELPRO) against civil rights and black liberation groups, the women's liberation movement, and other (mostly leftist) causes?

The most likely reason for these oversights, and for the preoccupation of four of the contributors to this volume with the defensive actions of protest movements, is their animosity toward these groups and ideologies revealed by their own words.

Gordon proclaims himself "fortunate, because Johns Hopkins is a small university . . . where the usual proportion of radicals is too few in absolute numbers to achieve critical mass." Jeffery suggests, perhaps jocularly, "From this fall from Eden, we now have creeping socialism and the feminist movement." Levin laments, "One mentions the crime rate of black adolescents with trepidation and apologies. Feminism, which has almost become our state religion, is similarly immune to scientific questioning." Henson asserts, "The fact is that women have not been and are not now victims of male oppression."

Their articles do not prove that sociobiology, racial differences in crime rates, and the influence of feminist gains on female criminality are tabooed topics, but instead demonstrate that objectivity still eludes many social scientists.

C. Ray Jeffery replies:

After reading the articles in this book, I wish to add several thoughts concerning the issue of research taboos.

I am especially disturbed by some of the conclusions in Professor Karmen's paper. He cites from a selective perspective of history the uses made of genetics to foster racism, elitism, and racist ideology. He ignores the fact that most of modern behavioral genetics is a product of biochemistry and the work of Watson and Crick in 1954. To cite early theories of criminology or genetics as being wrong is certainly not a recognition of what modern biology can contribute to criminology, nor is our earlier ignorance of genetics a reason for not doing research now.

Karmen states that there are no taboos on research into IQ and genetics, and then he cites in Table 1 a number of statements from organizations which in essence are intimidating to the researcher. He concludes with a statement from the National Academy of Sciences (1967) that argues that research in the IQ-genetics area is dangerous because the results of such research are ambiguous and could be misused by others. Karmen notes that the American Psychological Association in its 1972 resolution supported research into the role of heredity in behavior. He does not, however, list the APA resolution in Chart I where he cites evidence in support of limiting research in the area of genetics. For the record, I would like to quote from the 1972 APA resolution: "We have investigated much evidence concerning the possible role of inheritance in human abilities and behaviors, and we believe such hereditary influences are very strong. We wish strongly to encourage research into the biological hereditary bases of behavior as a major complement to the environmental efforts at explanation."

Karmen does not mention the 1951 UNESCO resolution that is probably the most famous resolution in this area. This resolution was not accepted by many of the geneticists on the panel, including Fisher, Darlington, Dobzhansky, and Medawar. These geneticists were critical of theories that deny or ignore genetic diversity (Vernon, 1979: 249).

Karmen cites Sagarin's statement on the right of social deviants not to be researched (also cited by Sagarin in his introductory remarks). This statement must be greatly qualified in order to be of use to criminologists. I have a right not to be researched if I have heart disease or cancer. I can die or receive treatment as I choose. However, if I have a contagious disease, if I want to drive while in an intoxicated condition, or if I have a brain tumor which causes uncontrollable violence, then I have no right to privacy. Crime by definition is a public act. As I have noted elsewhere, we are caught in an idiotic situation today in which we can legally execute people for behavior problems but we cannot legally treat them. Is there a "right to treatment'' doctrine for criminals? Does the public have a right to demand treatment for a dangerous person? If we can invade a person's privacy in order to execute him, we can invade his privacy in order to do research. Is our lack of understanding of human behavior and our inability to treat criminals successfully in any way related to our refusal to do research in controversial areas? How do we know why people behave as they do if we do not do the necessary research?

Karmen also cites Geis (1965) to the effect that racial identity should not be a matter of public record. Some of us 1950-style liberals (now called neoconservatives) remember the times when we fought successfully against attempts to have race included on college admissions applications and personnel applications. Now, as a part of our affirmative action effort, we must list sex and race of applicants for jobs and college admissions. Universities now have affirmative action officers, and universities are under court orders to admit more minority students or to hire more minority candidates.

We now bus black students many miles in order that they can sit next to white students. This is based on the assumptions that all individuals are alike and that all that differs are the school environments. If we had a rule that stated that all students with an IQ over 130 were to be bused to one school and all students with an IQ below 80 bused to another school, then busing would be on the basis of ability and not skin color. If a black female is not bused to a special program for gifted children when her IQ is above 130, then this is discrimination because of an identification of skin color with ability. If we assume a person's IQ from skin color, this is a misuse of genetics.

If we bus school children on the basis of skin color or if we hire people on the basis of skin color rather than ability, it is selection on the basis of race and not ability, and as such it is discriminatory. It is the liberal sociologist who supports educational and hiring policies based on skin color rather than ability who is perpetuating the race myth, not the geneticist.

Finally, since so much of this volume concerns the issue of genes and IQ, let me state my position once again, based on the best reading of modern behavioral genetics of which I am capable.

All phenotypic traits are a result of the interaction of genes and environment. An environment has to have something upon which to act. There can be no trait without a gene for the trait. IQ is a phenotypic trait, a product of genes and environment in interaction. An IQ score can be changed by variation in the genetic system and/or by variation in the environmental system. Genetic diversity is a part of natural selection and is needed for successful adaptation. With the exception of MZ (identical) twins who inherit the same genetic materials, no two individuals are genetically alike. Since genetic variation is much greater than environmental variation, for most people genetic variation plays a greater role in IQ than environmental variation.

The interaction of genes and environment can be found in the fact that a given genotype will have a wide range of effects in different environments; in other words, the expression of genes is determined by the environments in which they develop.

The closer individuals are genetically, the closer they are in IQ. MZ twins reared apart in different environments have a coefficient of .75, whereas unrelated individuals reared in the same environment have a coefficient of .24 (Vernon: 1979: 169).

IQ is mediated by the brain and the central nervous system. Genes do not produce IQ; genes produce protein synthesis, which leads to cell development, which leads to brains and nervous systems. The shape of the brain is a result of the interaction of genotype and environment, and environmental deficiencies or disease can produce an inferior brain, as in the case of stress, protein deficiencies, and other dietary and environmental deficiencies.

The "black box" approach to IQ—that is, measuring a response without knowing what is going on inside the brain—has always been a methodological problem in psychometrics. Today, it is suggested that IQ tests move inside the brain and measure evoked electric potentials and neural functioning. This approach would view IQ as an information-processing problem, which view is similar to those expressed in the work of neurologists such as Karl Pribram, who regards memory and learning as information-processing problems (Rice, 1979: 26; Vernon, 1979: 43ff.).

Jensen found a 15-point difference in the average of IQ scores of blacks and whites, of which he attributes .80 to genetic variability. This statement in itself does not deny the interaction of genes and environment or the overlap of IQ scores between black and white populations (Vernon, 1979: 13ff.).

The figure of .80 for genetic variation is based on the concept of *heritability*. Heritability, or h^2, is defined as the proportion of variance due to variation in genotypes. Total variation in phenotypes (Vt) is a result of variations in the environment (Ve) plus variations in the genotypes (Vg), or Vt = Ve + Vg. The phenotype is thus defined as the product of genetic variation and environmental variation. The formula for heritability is h^2 = Vg/Vt, or the ratio of genetic variation to total variation. From this we can see that the larger the Ve, the smaller the Vg. If one is dealing with pure inbred genetic strains, then Vg equals 0 and h^2 equals 0. If there is no genetic variability, then heritability is 0. If environmental variability is 0, then Ve is 0 and h^2 is 1. To say that Vg is 0 or Ve is 0 is not to say that there is no genetic influence or no environmental effect. It is obviously impossible to have corn without seeds and without soil, water, and sun. What the concept of heritability means is that the greater the variability in the genetic structure of a given population, the greater the heritability figure. The concept of heritability has been used by Jensen, Jencks, and others, and it is often misunderstood by social scientists (Vernon, 1979: 201 ff.; Halsey, 1977; McClearn and DeFries, 1973; Loehlin et al., 1975).

Heritability is a population statistic, not a trait property. Heritability refers to a given population in a given environment. Change the environment, and heritability changes. As we noted, when environmental variation is minimal, heritability is high. Such a statistical concept tells us no more about the trait in an individual member of the population than an average height of American males tells us the height of Johnny Jones. Heritability does not imply fixed IQ, nor does it imply that teaching and learning are unimportant. Heritability does not mean IQ is cast in stone.

The politics of modern genetics is confused, to say the least. At one point in history, liberal political thought was based on the recognition and preservation of individual differences. To be different did not mean to be inferior. Now, liberal political thought is based on an egalitarianism which destroys any concept of individuality or individual differences. We always cite the Nazi movement in our condemnation of genetics research, while we ignore the pure environmentalism of the communists and Lysenko. The Russians cannot grow wheat with their environmentalist doctrines. We would do well to pause in our haste to condemn research and ask why both ends of the political spectrum—fascism and communism—led to tragic results. Perhaps freedom to do research is an essential ingredient missing in all forms of tyranny. If biological facts offend us, then let us at least be aware of our assumptions about the nature of man.

REFERENCES

HALSEY, A. H. [ed.] (1977) Heredity and Environment. New York: Macmillan.
LOEHLIN, J., G. LINDZEY, and J. N. SPUHLER (1975) Race Differences in Intelligence. San Francisco: Freeman.
McCLEARN, G. E. and J. C. DeFRIES (1973) Introduction to Behavioral Genetics. San Francisco: Freeman.
RICE, B. (1979) "Brave new world of intelligence testing." Psychology Today (September): 27-41.
VERNON, P. (1979) Intelligence: Heredity and Environment. San Francisco: Freeman.

Robert A. Gordon replies:

Sagarin's remarks in his introduction to this volume place me in a quandary. How am I to remonstrate with a host who elsewhere has been supportive of some of my research and with whom I have enjoyed a cordial and stimulating correspondence, conducted with mutual respect? Perhaps he will not mind my divulging the fact that he himself has spontaneously expressed second thoughts concerning the tone of some of his criticisms in the introduction and has even offered to soften them if I found them too objectionable. That is a generous offer indeed, but it is never a policy of mine to request such changes. Instead, it may prove more instructive for bystanders to this controversy and others like it if Sagarin's remarks are allowed to stand and if I attempt to take them behind the scenes a bit, as I see matters, in accordance with the spirit of my somewhat informal essay earlier in this volume.

Sagarin has impressed me as a man with a deep devotion to the principles of science—witness other remarks in his introduction as well as his sponsorship of this symposium—who has long championed certain moral causes. Recent work by myself and others seems to threaten those causes by challenging the conceptions on which they have been based. Although Sagarin clearly recognizes our right to do this, and even acknowledges the potential benefits of the process, there is no mistaking the fact that it troubles him deeply and makes him angry at times.

Sagarin's present introduction contrasts with the extremely fair discussion of my work prepared under his supervision for the recent revision of Vold's (1979) classic criminology text, in which even Shockley, everyone's bête noire, reveives a far more objective treatment than one is accustomed to seeing. True, the Vold chapter ends on a disapproving and skeptical note, but I could not ask for a more accurate presentation of my work, which at least puts the reader of that volume in a position to think for himself. The overall effect is certainly a far cry from the more negative assessment of the IQ-delinquency question offered by Vold while he was alive.

I would much rather face occasional flashes of anger from a man of fundamental integrity caught between conflicting principles than try to reason with a cooler ideologue who gives only lip service to the ideal of open inquiry. Sagarin believes in science—and this costs him anguish. It is important for readers to realize, students especially, that behind such fierce language as Sagarin employs in his introduction there is often more respect for opposing arguments than the angry words would lead one to expect.

I would not have guessed, for example, had Sagarin not volunteered this in personal communication, that he views his statement concerning me, "But he may be right, after all," as balancing off his negative comments and, I daresay, neither would most other readers. Apparently, this particular sentence constitutes a significant concession to scientific discipline from Sagarin's troubled standpoint, and I am now inclined to read his angry remarks as a manifestation of the other side of his ambivalence seeking expression. The lesson is that the rational argument neither resides in the indignation nor is indexed by it. A scientific attitude toward bland topics is easily maintained—the test of our ideals always occurs in connection with extreme cases (as is often pointed out when the Supreme Court, for example, frees an obvious criminal over a technical omission by police).

My sympathy for Sagarin's personal conflict does not oblige me to remain silent concerning matters of fact in evident need of clarification, however. Indeed, our mutual respect depends on such clarification.

Let me deal first with some points concerning the role of Burt's work. Although Sagarin appears to be under the impression that the correlation between IQ and delinquency "required fraud to validate," this is the first such specific allegation against Burt's delinquency research that I have heard, and Sagarin presents no evidence. Second, I did not "lean" on Shockley; I merely cited him because he had scientific priority with an analysis similar to mine. I was, as a matter of fact, a bit disappointed to discover his priority, which, from a political standpoint, it would have been expedient for me to ignore. Sagarin's remark about Shockley's "reliability" is gratuitous, for neither he nor anyone else has proven Shockley dishonest or his major hypothesis wrong. Had this been the case, the furor would have ended long ago. Third, when I did cite Burt (1961) exclusively, it had to do with his "numerical example" (as I put it) of intergenerational regression to the IQ mean. This was only for incidental didactic purposes. Although that particular paper of Burt's is suspect (Dorfman, 1978), the phenomenon of regression is well established and not dependent on Burt. Fourth, Shockley (1967) did not "depend" on Burt either, but did obtain a somewhat better fit for extreme data points using a nonnormal IQ distribution in one of his models that Burt had advanced: Had Shockley ignored that distribution, which differs from the normal mainly beyond two standard deviations from the mean, his presentation would have been somewhat less thorough. No one thus far has cast serious doubt on the potential plausibility of such a nonnormal distribution. Jensen (1980: 120), who has pointed out many anomalies in Burt's data (Jensen, 1974), still refers to this distribution by citing the same paper of Burt's. Because the difference in distributions is slight in the IQ range of interest, I have employed the normal approximation in my own work. Fifth, at least six sets of authors have noted that Burt's now discredited kinship data were in good agreement with other bodies of similar data and hence not crucial for establishing the heritability of IQ (Wade, 1976; Rimland and Munsinger, 1977; Rowe and Plomin, 1978; Jensen, 1978: 15-16; Eysenck, 1979; Cronbach, 1979). To a substantial degree, this good agreement accounts for earlier failures to challenge Burt's integrity.

A more efficient and productive dialogue would ensue if critics would confine themselves to main issues and points truly essential to the argument. However, Burt's misdeeds are now frequently employed as a distractor or red herring in IQ-related debates, and it is not uncommon to receive an audience-oriented lecture about Burt as a response to any utterance concerning IQ, however remote it may be from Burt in actual substance. Some people, apparently, would rather keep their opponents talking about Burt.

Sagarin's impression that the IQ-delinquency correlation was "fabricated out of whole cloth" in the work of Burt may owe much to the widely publicized claims of Kamin (1977, 1978; Rensberger, 1977), who exaggerates the degree to which the behavioral genetic position depended on Burt's results and questions all of Burt's earlier research as well. Kamin has informed reporters that "Burt's purported findings went largely unchallenged for decades because the data could be taken as scientific evidence that blacks are inherently intellectually inferior to whites" (Rensberger, 1977: 44). In actuality, Burt (1969: 228) expressed doubt that heredity was substantially involved in the black-white IQ difference. (Apparently, his data did not of themselves serve the purpose Kamin claims.) Kamin (1978) has informed the public that 99 black infants adopted into privileged white families later obtained an average IQ of 110.4. But here he withheld the key fact from newspaper readers, as Mercer (1977: 1643-1644, 1655) did from the judge in the Larry P case, that 68 of the 99 "black" adoptees had had one natural parent who was white (Scarr and Weinberg, 1976: Table 10). Black adoptees whose natural parents were both black exhibited at most a 6.8 point gain over their locally expected IQ of 90. Although sampling artifacts cannot be ruled out entirely, even if this gain were real it would not be at all inconsistent with substantial heritability for IQ, in view of the extreme and intensive nature of the environmental intervention (e.g., Jensen, 1973). From time to time, Kamin has identified genuine shortcomings in IQ research, but he is far from being a dependable interpreter of IQ literature, as these examples demonstrate, and readers would do well to consult the penetrating review of Kamin's (1974) book by Fulker (1975) before accepting everything Kamin claims.

The most convincing case against Burt has been assembled, with help from Burt's own diary, by his biographer, Hearnshaw (1979). Some fabrication of data certainly occurred, but this may have represented an egotistic attempt to compensate for material lost in wartime bombing, and Burt evidently took care not to stray far from values previously published by others (see also Cronbach, 1979). But Hearnshaw (1979: 286) regards Burt's work up to the late 1930s as basically sound. He also concludes that Burt was a skilled clinician with extensive exposure to delinquents both in his own childhood and later professional career, and asserts that Burt's (1925) work on delinquency was perhaps his best book (Hearnshaw, 1979: 39, 271-273, 77). Neither Shockley nor I drew on Burt's delinquency book, although in other work I have quoted some of Burt's astute clinical comments that appear there. Consequently, I am at a loss to account for Sagarin's remarks about Burt. If he has been misled by Kamin, it may interest him to know that one of the unpublished letters to the *New York Times* referred to in my earlier chapter was written in an attempt to dispel misimpressions left by Kamin.

Two of Sagarin's criticisms strike me as petty and irrelevant to any argument of consequence. If I had thought it necessary to "establish" the New Left inclinations of the *New York Times,* I certainly would not have rested with citing Podhoretz, whom I respect greatly but do not consider infallible. I simply noted his view of the editorial opinion page of the *Times* in passing, and readers could take it for whatever it was worth. Many persons would regard Podhoretz as a well-positioned and discerning informant concerning the New York intellectual scene, but apparently Sagarin does not. Of course, I too read the *Times* and am capable of forming my own opinion, although I do not think mine would be considered as authoritative as Podhoretz's. If the Op-Ed page does not reflect a New Left bias, how does it lean? Toward the Right, the Old Left, or Dead Center? With Tom Wicker as associate editor?

It is interesting to note that a rather inoffensive opinion identifying a newspaper with the New Left draws such a harsh response from our host, whereas Karmen's unsubtle identification of his scientific opponents with the Ku Klux Klan elicits no reaction at all. I am also sorry to learn that one cannot describe one's own research as having a successful outcome without being accused of immodesty. It had been my impression that scientists made such judgments routinely whenever they switched to a next topic. Both of these lapses, no doubt, serve to establish my lack of qualifications for conducting research on topics offensive to Sagarin.

Sagarin seems to feel that for my 1976 article to be tolerated, it must be of "impeccable quality," which places me in danger of being termed immodest again if I attempt to defend it. Having decided to convert an occasion for discussing taboos into one for discussing the quality of my substantive work—which is not before the reader in this volume—Sagarin should have concentrated on important issues. Instead, we are offered much sarcasm and innuendo, and a description of my work that is barely recognizable to me. I invite the reader to consult the original (Gordon, 1976) and also the more faithful description in Vold (1979). Ambiguous phrases such as "studies which he reinterprets to suit his own needs" could refer to the fact that I reanalyzed data from some studies, adjusted some to a common age basis, and so on—or to something worse. Let us assume that if Sagarin means that I *misinterpreted* some studies, he would not have neglected to provide specific details.

In reducing my eighty-page article to five platitudes, Sagarin manages to omit the fact that my analysis showed many delinquency rates of whites to be remarkably stable over a wide range of communities and times (just as IQ parameters would be), and several corresponding but higher rates for blacks to be closely commensurate with the magnitude of the mean IQ difference between blacks and whites. Both of these points appeared as two of a numbered series of six arguments supporting the relevance of IQ to delinquency in my article (Gordon, 1976: 257-265). Sagarin's five propositions overlap these six arguments in part but also depart from them in curious ways, in view of his disturbing claim that "most" of the propositions were "made with little or no validation whatsoever."

Let us examine Sagarin's list in light of this serious allegation. The two omitted points just discussed were key ones based on important data presented in my article itself. Sagarin's first proposition, that black males have higher delinquency rates than white males, does not represent these two points adequately, although it can certainly be subsumed into them. Sagarin's third point, that blacks have a lower mean IQ than whites, was supported by several citations—including one to a prior review by me (Gordon, 1975a) which, in turn, cited other concurring reviews—to the validity of the race difference. Sagarin is quite familiar with that article of mine, which has since been updated (Gordon and Rudert, 1979; Gordon, 1980; see also the monumental review by Jensen, 1980). The fourth of Sagarin's points, that IQ is (substantially) inherited, and its empirically established corollary that close kinship correlations are heavily positive, was supported by citations to major reviews by Jensen that have held up well over time despite the Burt situation. I employed heritability to account for adoption data, suggesting that criminality has a genetic component, as well as for the intergenerational stability of IQ. Although a just-published review (Plomin and DeFries, 1980: 21-22) reports heritabilities from later studies as being "closer to .50 than .70," its authors also state that they "know of no specific environmental influences nor combinations of them that account for as much as 10 percent of the variance in IQ." This means that known genetic causes are at least five times more potent than known environmental causes in determining IQ.

Sagarin's fifth proposition finds its way onto his list from an altogether different part of my article, where I introduced it as follows: "In theory, for example, the low IQ child-low IQ parent dyad is fraught with potential for poor socialization outcomes" (Gordon, 1976: 269). Thus, what was plainly identified as a purely theoretical proposition has been inserted into a list that purportedly summarizes my empirical basis for linking race, IQ, and delinquency, where it serves to bolster the charge that I presented insufficient evidence for the propositions. All the other propositions reviewed above—except the inappropriate fifth—had been accompanied by ample empirical evidence. I can also add that I have a book-length manuscript in progress, based on my own research in part, that will lend substantial support to the fifth point on Sagarin's list.

Thus far, I have skipped over Sagarin's second point, namely, that delinquents have lower IQs than nondelinquents, because it represents a special case. I introduced this particular proposition into my list of six arguments with both a special warning and a promise: "I am well aware that this last statement flies in the face of literature which contends or seems to show that IQ is not related to delinquency. At some future time I will treat that literature" (Gordon, 1976: 257). I presented this one argument in such an explicitly cursory manner because nothing I could say in the space available would have been adequate to deal with the issues I had in mind, and simply citing all or a few of the many studies I had collected would have been unavailing. In a later paper (Gordon, 1975b), I did discuss a few of the issues, but soon after, Hirschi and Hindelang (1977) published an excellent article that accomplished exactly what I had intended and more, so I did not bother to write the article I had promised. Sagarin is well aware of the article by Hirschi and Hindelang—it is discussed next to mine in the Vold (1979) volume that he supervised.

We see, therefore, that all of the propositions on Sagarin's list except the inappropriate fifth one that was intended to play a purely theoretical role—as well as others his list ignores completely—were accompanied by empirical evidence sufficient to justify scientific publication by usual standards, by citations to such evidence, or (in the one case) by a promise of evidence that was filled by others before I could accomplish the task myself. Moreover, when a number of varied and independent arguments converge on the same conclusion in science, the strength of the whole is usually considered to be greater than that of the individual components summed.

In view of my explicit enumeration of the key arguments for my position, it is unfair of Sagarin to have assembled a different and less convincing list of his own, which he then uses to impugn the quality of my evidence. I do not find this style of criticism either scientific or productive. Perhaps when he is less angry, Sagarin will not either. Right before us, I believe, we have an example of the distortions that unchecked emotion can introduce into the perception and evaluation of evidence—even by a man of Sagarin's integrity. Suppose that Sagarin had been refereeing my article for a journal anonymously, or worse yet, weighing a research proposal that typically consisted more of hypotheses than of evidence, and you will understand more about research taboos and their effects than any amount of abstract argument can possibly convey.

Whatever its source, the straw man with which Sagarin replaces my arguments sets the stage for converting a scientific issue into a moral one, where Sagarin apparently feels on surer ground. I, personally, would be more impressed if he had arrived at this juncture by a less tendentious route. Nevertheless, let us give the remainder of Sagarin's argument serious attention, since in principle it need not depend on whether or not his prior description of my research was objectively sound.

His remaining argument can be stated as a rough syllogism with two premises and a conclusion. I rushed "headlong into print," the findings were dangerous ones; ergo, I was irresponsible. It is important to remind readers that a syllogism can be valid without being true, and therefore it is essential to examine the premises.

First of all, we have no dependable criteria for assessing what constitutes rushing into print (hence the utility of belittling my evidence earlier). This charge was directed at Jensen too, but his 1969 paper has triggered an international revival of research on genetics and intelligence and has held up well over the years. Apparently, that judgment of hastiness was itself hasty. One can imagine subjective judgments being rendered by panels of judges, either before publication or after, but such panels would spell the end of the free exchange of ideas that enables science to thrive, and they beg the question concerning the validity of the judgments. Furthermore, each of any two sides could employ such panels to denounce the other. It is much better that scientists save their energy for tasks amenable to their special qualifications than descend into the murky business of prejudging ideas as hasty and dangerous.

One implication of Sagarin's position concerning supposed haste is that controversial ideas and hypotheses should not be shared with the general scientific community. Responding to similar attacks on Jensen, Cronbach (1975: 6) commented dryly, "One infers that the social scientist with a disturbing hypothesis should pursue it privately, keeping his dark suspicions secret until he has a solid case. Given the social nature of the scientific enterprise, this seems as inhospitable to heterodoxy as an outright embargo on a research topic."

Sagarin's argument concerning dangerousness can be, and often is, made separately. It gains credence from the fact that most important ideas can be portrayed as dangerous, and ideas concerning IQ are no exceptions. If this were not the case, the historical issue of censorship and freedom of speech would never have arisen. However, neither Sagarin nor Karmen has a monopoly on the ability to perceive danger. I claim to be at least their equal in assessing danger to blacks and whites, and there are other scenarios, undreamt of in my critics' philosophies, that depict our citizens as being in far greater danger from each other if IQ differences between races remain both stubborn and substantial, as they have remained since World War I (Gordon, forthcoming). According to those scenarios, ignoring the matter only exacerbates the danger. There is a sociopolitics of IQ, but it is opposite in causal direction to the one imagined by Kamin (1974), and it can foster extremism at either end of the political spectrum even if IQ is never mentioned. The best way to prevent irresponsible use of ideas is by making responsible and honest use of them. "In the welter of conflicting fanaticisms, one of the few unifying forces is scientific truthfulness . . . producing, wherever it exists, a lessening of fanaticism with an increasing capacity of sympathy and mutual understanding" (Russell, 1945: 836).

Herrnstein (1980: 48) has remarked, correctly in my opinion, "IQ is often the silent partner in standard sociological and economic explanations of many aspects of society." Standard explanations, therefore, are not likely to lead to true understanding if the silent partner plays an active role; quite the contrary, they are apt to frustrate solutions and aggravate grievances and thus enhance the prospect of social conflict as good will and lead time are squandered. Those who place high-minded objections in the way of frank discussion ought to realize that they are not the only ones capable of moral vision. As Wilson (1976: 190) so clearly observed when replying to certain critics of sociobiology, "Knowledge humanely acquired and widely shared, related to human needs but kept free of political censorship, is the real science for the people."

REFERENCES

BURT, C. (1925) The Young Delinquent. London: Univ. of London Press.
——— (1961) "Intelligence and social mobility." British J. of Stat. Psychology 14: 3-24.
——— (1969) "Intelligence and heredity." The New Scientist 42: 226-228.

CRONBACH, L. J. (1975) "Five decades of public controversy over mental testing." Amer. Psychologist 30: 1-14.

——— (1979) "Hearnshaw on Burt." Science 206: 1392-1394.

DORFMAN, D. D. (1978) "The Cyril Burt question: new findings." Science 201: 1177-1186.

EYSENCK, H. J. (1979) The Structure and Measurement of Intelligence. New York: Springer-Verlag.

FULKER, D. W. (1975) Review of "The Science and Politics of IQ," by L. J. Kamin. Amer. J. of Psychology 88: 505-519.

GORDON, R. A. (1975a) "Examining labelling theory: the case of mental retardation," pp. 83-146 in W. R. Gove (ed.) The Labelling of Deviance: Evaluating a Perspective. Beverly Hills, CA: Sage Publications.

——— (1975b) "Crime and cognition: an evolutionary perspective." Proceedings of the Second International Symposium on Criminology. São Paulo, Brazil: Oscar Freire Institute.

——— (1976) "Prevalence: the rare datum in delinquency measurement and its implications for the theory of delinquency," pp. 201-284 in M. W. Klein (ed.) The Juvenile Justice System. Beverly Hills, CA: Sage Publications.

——— (1980) "Labelling theory, mental retardation, and public policy: Larry P. and other developments since 1974," pp. 175-225 in W. R. Gove (ed.) The Labelling of Deviance: Evaluating a Perspective. Beverly Hills, CA: Sage Publications.

——— (forthcoming) "Implications of valid (and stubborn) IQ differences: an unstatesmanlike view." Behavioral and Brain Sciences.

——— and E. E. RUDERT (1979) "Bad news concerning IQ tests." Sociology of Education 52: 174-190.

HEARNSHAW, L. S. (1979) Cyril Burt, Psychologist. Ithaca, NY: Cornell Univ. Press.

HERRNSTEIN, R. J. (1980) "In defense of intelligence tests." Commentary 69 (February): 40-51.

HIRSCHI, T. and M. J. HINDELANG (1977) "Intelligence and delinquency: a revisionist review." Amer. Soc. Rev. 42: 572-587.

JENSEN, A. R. (1973) "Let's understand Skodak and Skeels, finally." Educ. Psychologist 10: 30-35.

——— (1974) "Kinship correlations reported by Sir Cyril Burt." Behavior Genetics 4: 1-28.

——— (1978) "The current status of the IQ controversy." Australian Psychologist 13: 7-27.

——— (1980) Bias in Mental Testing. New York: Macmillan.

KAMIN, L. J. (1974) The Science and Politics of I.Q. New York: John Wiley.

——— (1977) "Burt's IQ data." Science 195: 246-248.

——— (1978) "The I.Q. controversy." The Baltimore Sun (November 25): A12.

MERCER, J. R. (1977) "Expert witness testimony." Reporters' Daily Transcript, Larry P. et al. v. Wilson Riles et al., United States District Court, Northern District of California.

PLOMIN, R. and J. C. DeFRIES (1980) "Genetics and intelligence: recent data." Intelligence 4: 15-24.

RENSBERGER, B. (1977) "Fraud in research is a rising problem in science." New York Times (January 23): 1, 44.

RIMLAND, B. and H. MUNSINGER (1977) "Burt's IQ data." Science 195: 248.

ROWE, D. and R. PLOMIN (1978) "The Burt controversy: a comparison of Burt's data on IQ with data from other studies." Behavior Genetics 8: 81-83.

RUSSELL, B. (1945) A History of Western Philosophy. New York: Simon & Schuster.

SCARR, S. and R. A. WEINBERG (1976) "IQ test performance of black children adopted by white families." Amer. Psychologist 31: 726-739.

SHOCKLEY, W. (1967) "A 'try simplest cases' approach to the heredity-poverty-crime problem." Proceedings of the National Academy of Sciences 57: 1767-1774.

VOLD, G. B. (1979) Theoretical Criminology. New York: Oxford Univ. Press.

WADE, N. (1976) "IQ and heredity: suspicion of fraud beclouds classic experiment." Science 194: 916-919.

WILSON, E. O. (1976) "Academic vigilantism and the political significance of sociobiology." BioScience 26: 183, 187-190.

Edward Sagarin replies:

It would be inappropriate and unfair for me to reply to Gordon's rebuttal, so he shall have the last word in this volume, but not in the debate. For that, I refer the readers to the article by Gordon against which I argued so strongly (not angrily, just strongly) and to my essay in this volume and his reply; all will judge for themselves.

There are a few minor points that do require clarification, for they are now introduced at a late date into the argument. Some people would separate Burt into two beings, the honest one and the dishonest one. I go by the rule of law in a courtroom, that if one disbelieves a witness in any particular, one can choose to disbelieve that witness in all other respects. I do not see how Burt can still be cited for some of his work when he proved not to be wrong, but to be a fake in other work. And, to reiterate, if scientific principles did not demand such a stance on my part, prudence would.

The question of IQ of children of mixed black and white parentage has been introduced. Almost all anthropological studies of black Americans have concluded that they contain a large amount of white ancestry; Melville Herskovits believed that at least 80% of blacks were part white, many of them more white than black. I know of no IQ studies that have correlated alleged black inferiority with racial ancestry, although this should be crucial.

For those authors who have cited my work on the right not to be researched, please note that I deny the right of privacy from research for publicly accountable groups (such as thieves, rapists, and Pentagon officials, among others).

ABOUT THE AUTHORS

ROBERT A. GORDON is Associate Professor of Social Relations at Johns Hopkins University. He received his Ph.D. from the University of Chicago in 1963. His major research interests are in the social psychology of deviant behavior, values, small group interaction, opiate addiction, sociology of intelligence, causes of crime and delinquency, and socialization. He is the author of numerous articles and in 1974 shared the American Association for the Advancement of Science Socio-Psychological Prize for work on opiate addiction.

S. DEON HENSON was director of the Peter W. Rodino Institute of Criminal Justice from 1976 to 1979. She has taught at Kean College and at Rutgers, has written on sentencing and on juvenile justice, among other subjects, and is currently working on two projects, a study of anorexia and a work tentatively entitled "The Myth of Rule by Law."

C. RAY JEFFERY obtained his Ph.D. from Indiana University, where he was a student of the late Edwin Sutherland. After postdoctoral fellowships in law and social science at the University of Chicago and the University of Wisconsin, he taught at Arizona State, the Washington School of Psychiatry, and New York University, and he is currently Professor of Criminology at Florida State University. He is coauthor of *Society and the Law,* author of *Criminal Responsibility and Mental Disease* and *Crime Prevention through Environmental Design,* and editor of *Biology and Crime.* He served as editor of *Criminology,* vice-president and president of the American Society of Criminology, was a Fulbright-Hays Scholar, and is presently working in the areas of biology, psychology, learning theory, and criminology.

ANDREW KARMEN received his Ph.D. from Columbia University in 1977 and is Assistant Professor of Sociology at the John Jay College of Criminal Justice of the City University of New York. He has written articles on agents provocateurs, drug addiction, automobile theft, blackout looting, and is currently working on a book on victimology.

MICHAEL E. LEVIN is Professor of Philosophy at City College and City University of New York. He is the author of *Metaphysics and the Mind-Body Problem* (Oxford, 1979) and articles on the foundations of mathematics, the philosophy of science, and ethics (many coauthored with his wife). He is currently working on the definability of arithmetical truth in higher-order languages and is preparing a paper on whether racial discrimination is a morally serious wrong.

EDWARD SAGARIN is Professor of Sociology at City College and City University of New York and will be University Distinguished Visiting Professor at Ohio State University during part of the 1980-1981 academic year. He is a former president of the American Society of Criminology, was coeditor with Donal E. J. MacNamara of its journal *Criminology,* and editor of *Deviance and Social Change* (a Sage publication in an annual series). He is coauthor with MacNamara of *Sex, Crime, and the Law* (Macmillan, 1978) and author of *Raskolnikov and Others: Literary Images of Crime, Punishment, Redemption and Atonement* (St. Martin's, 1980).